CHINA
in *change*

DAVID MONEY

Hodder & Stoughton

A MEMBER OF THE HODDER HEADLINE GROUP

Acknowledgements
The author and publishers thank the following for permission
to reproduce photographs in this book.
J Allan Cash *Figures* 3.30, 6.8; Robert Harding *Figures* 3.11, 3.29,
5.1, 5.25, 5.27, 5.40, 6.28; Michael Morrish *Figures* F, 3.15, 3.24,
3.32, 5.36, 5.37, 5.38; Geoffrey Sherlock *Figures* 3.23, 3.34,
6.20, 6.26. All other photos belong to the Author.
Every effort has been made to trace and acknowledge correctly
all copyright holders but if any have been overlooked the
publishers will be pleased to make the necessary arrangements
at the first opportunity.
All figures were correct at the time of going to press.

British Library Cataloguing in Publication Data

ISBN 0 340 65515 1

First published 1996
Impression number 10 9 8 7 6 5 4 3 2 1
Year 1999 1998 1997 1996

Copyright © 1996 David Money

Typeset by Transet Limited, Coventry
Printed in Great Britain for Hodder & Stoughton Educational,
a division of Hodder Headline Plc,
338 Euston Road, London NW1 3BH
by Scotprint Ltd, Musselburgh

Contents

PART 1

The influence of natural features

PART 2

From Empire to Republic

PART 3

Rural-urban contrasts

Preface

Figure B Foreign investment in China has soared, and most new projects are joint Sino-foreign enterprises. Much investment, especially from Taiwan, is channelled through these Hong Kong business houses

Remarkable changes, affecting almost a quarter of the world's population and of increasing global significance, have been taking place in China. The social consequences of this are of prime interest to geographers and environmentalists, for China is achieving a high rate of economic growth, increasing foreign trade and investment and improving living standards for most of its huge population, yet also experiencing considerable problems related to such rapid reforms. Cities and specific zones targeted for Sino-foreign investment are experiencing strong economic growth and increasing population, attracting millions of people from less favoured parts of the country. Statistics related to urban population, and to the country's rising volume of trade and GDP, should be viewed in the light of rapid change.

This view of China in change presents a wide range of themes which geographers will find relevant to conditions in other parts of the world: people-environment inter-relationships, population growth and distribution; urbanisation; ethnic problems, push/pull factors of migration; pollution and deforestation; water shortages;

energy concerns; and impacts of tourism. These are seen in relation to China's remarkable physical structure, size, regional contrasts, and the experiences of a civilisation stretching back thousands of years. Its determination to progress by 'walking on two legs' by using both hi-tech inputs and intermediate technology gives a clear picture of the direction in which developing countries need to go.

For ease of reference, themes are presented in this book as separate topics, with cross-references and 'In Focus...' insets drawing attention to particular issues.

This introduction to China aims to give as clear a picture as possible of a country which, for various reasons, tends to be viewed only incidentally in the 'West', and hardly at all in the education system, yet is now the focus of international commercial and financial attention, and has increasing influence globally.

Figure A Karst pinnacles of the Stone Forest in Yunnan, one of China's many natural attractions. Each year millions of tourists provide a vital source of foreign currency

Introduction: past and present

China, unique in so many respects, is often regarded as a nation where rigid central control has imposed uniformity on its peoples and their ways of life; yet it is misleading to generalise about a country with such physical contrasts, massive population, variety of ethnic groups and diversity of living standards. Contrasting environmental conditions inevitably mean different lifestyles and opportunities for those in the tropical hill villages, in northern manufacturing cities with their bitter winters, for the millions farming the closely settled floodplains of central China and minority groups occupying desert oases thousands of kilometres to the west.

Policies aimed at meeting the general needs of some 1200 million people, nearly one-quarter of the world's population, may not necessarily enhance welfare and economic progress in all these contrasting regions. It is essential to appreciate the scales involved, and to consider the difficulties of administering 20 times the population of the United Kingdom within China's immense and often awkward terrain.

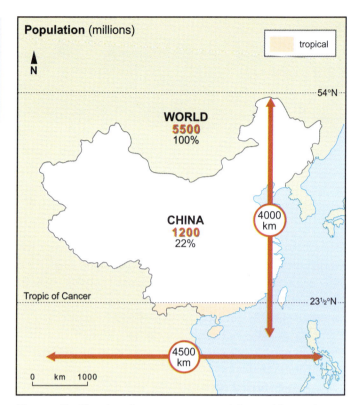

Figure D China has almost one-quarter of the world's population, in environments varying from the tropics to locations similar to eastern Canada

The time-scale, too, is relevant, for modern China owes much to its long history of civilisation. Organised societies controlled territories in the north as far back as 2000 BC and the Chinese Empire lasted from 221 BC to 1911. Invasions and revolutions created new dynasties, yet a remarkable continuity of social structure and practices persisted over the ages. Centuries before the Empire developed, ordered relationships between rulers and their people, between members of families and society, and between populations and natural forces had been considered by Confucius and other philosophers, and officially accepted as ideals. Later, a stable administrative system, using scholar officials, continued to preserve Chinese traditions, despite a succession of dynasties and changing boundaries.

The use of pictograph writing, the form of characters which can be understood by those who speak different languages, helped to control distant regions and introduce

Figure C An edifice near Luoyang which bridges 2000 years of civilisation. Beyond the spring wheat rises a 13-storey pagoda, built in the eleventh century at the site which 1000 years before received the first Buddhist scriptures from India

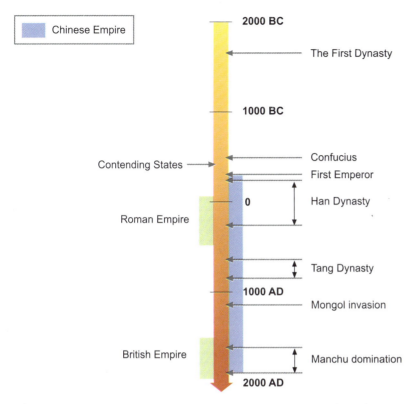

Chinese Empire

2000 BC

The First Dynasty

1000 BC

Contending States — Confucius
First Emperor

0 — Han Dynasty

Roman Empire

Tang Dynasty

1000 AD

Mongol invasion

British Empire — Manchu domination

2000 AD

Figure E The span of imperial rule, under which the continuity of social structure and administration owed much to Confucianism (see page 18)

Figure F Over the centuries foreign traders travelling the Silk Road paused at oases in western China (Figure 2.3). Today, travellers to Urumqi use an edifice which contrasts with that in Figure C, symbolising a rapidly changing China and the benefits of foreign investments

practical ways of doing things. Continuity is evident throughout China, where long-established methods of farming, terracing, wall-building, and processing raw materials have been handed down through generations. Cultural and family traditions have remained strong – though the effects of accelerating social changes are considered on page 15.

It is the history of the last 300 years, however, which is the key to assessing the achievements of this rapidly developing nation, and to appreciating its attitudes towards other countries. It is essential to understand the effects of the incursions and territorial acquisitions by foreign powers (page 22); their influences for self-advantage on the tottering Manchu Empire and their role in its eventual collapse. Foreign relationships with the powerful warlords, who soon dominated the new Republic, and subsequent foreign support for the Nationalists who, on coming to power, turned on the Communists who had assisted them, should also be appreciated. After 1936 a decade of conflict, partial occupation by Japan, and a bitter civil war preceded the establishment of **The People's Republic** in 1949. It inherited the consequent devastation and poverty, but apart from initial assistance from the USSR, the struggle to effect recovery through centrally controlled communal organisation remained unrecognised, with no aid from the

major foreign powers for over 20 years. Even though China now moves towards parity in technological and economic fields, such historic events must colour its views of Japan and the West, with whom it now deals financially, gaining technical expertise and attracting investment.

The introduction of a **socialist market system** and rapid industrialisation have proved economically successful on a national scale, though creating inflation, unemployment and population migration problems. Also, for the first time, there are wide differences in opportunities and lifestyles between individuals, and increasing contrasts between the poorer provinces, mainly in the west, and those favoured by natural conditions, coastal locations, and special economic privileges.

China's global relationships are also changing rapidly, with large-scale investment by foreign governments and international firms established in the cities. Increasing consumption by a growing population with rising living standards is bound to make heavier demands on world resources. This, of course, concerns us all, and makes it particularly important to understand as much as possible about this sizeable proportion of the world's population.

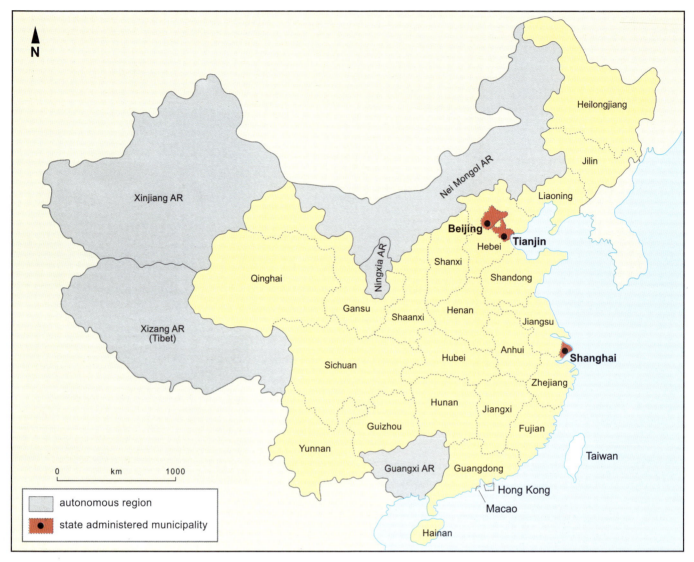

Figure G Political divisions

Provinces and Autonomous Regions

The government of The People's Republic of China (PRC) exercises authority through Provinces and five Autonomous Regions – Nei Mongol (Inner Mongolia), Ningxia, Xinjiang, Guangxi, and Xizang (Tibet), in which minority peoples have partial self-government. It also directly administers three Municipalities – Beijing, Tianjin, and Shanghai – each with considerable rural territory, helping to support a large urban core, and containing secondary settlements.

Hong Kong and Portuguese Macao will shortly become part of The People's Republic; but while Taiwan has growing economic relationships with the PRC, which regards it as Chinese territory (page 78), it retains its independence.

Place names and pronunciation

Chinese place names appear unfamiliar but are descriptive, each syllable adding to the meaning. Thus knowing that *bei, nan, dong,* and *xi* mean, respectively, north, south, east, and west, and that *he* is a river, *hu* a lake, and *shan* a mountain indicates why the provinces Shandong, Shanxi, Henan, Hebei, Hunan and Hubei are so named. Most place names tell of landscape features or local influences, and the glossary on page 90, provides translations of terms in common use.

In conversation tonal differences are crucial, but the following will help with pronunciation:
c – ts (as in 'bits'); e – ur (as in 'occur'); o – aw (as in 'law'); q – ch (as in 'chin'); x – sh (as in 'she'); zh – j (as in 'jack').

The influence of natural features

- A country of great physical contrasts

- A wide variety of climates

- Climate and rural activities

- Influences on population distribution

- Controlling a vast and diverse population

PART 1

A country of great physical contrasts

Figure 1.1 Deeply gullied loess with levelled brown fields prepared for planting spring wheat

China is a country of remarkable physical contrasts, with a North–South divide in mid-China, reflected by the distribution of population (page 13). To the west, mountain chains rise above the Tibetan massif, whose rugged plateau surface is 3500 m above sea level. To the east, amid lower, eroded mountains, are potentially fertile river basins, plains, and wide deltas. There is less variation in altitude in the north, with mountain-fringed western basins at 400 m, and the Turpan depression 150 m *below* sea-level. At this latitude climatic conditions make for East–West contrasts: the eastern lowlands receive considerable summer rain, whereas westwards, it becomes progressively drier, with interior deserts experiencing temperature extremes.

Patterns of highland and lowland

Some 30 million years ago successive crustal movements slowly raised the Tibetan Plateau, folding the Himalayan ranges against its southern flank. Long before this, crustal movements had created mountain ranges in eastern Asia which, though greatly eroded, are dominant features throughout China, enclosing lowland basins and diverting the drainage systems of the major rivers.

The trends of these earlier ranges are shown, in simplified form, in Figure 1.2. Subsequent weathering, erosion and, in some cases, uplift have produced a variety of relief forms, from the snowy peaks of the Kunlun Shan, rising to over 7000 m, to the lower, dissected mountains and broken hill country of eastern China, which nevertheless form dramatic scenery.

East of the great massif are lower plateaux with distinctive landforms. The Yunnan Plateau in the south west is deeply dissected by southward-flowing rivers and by tributaries draining eastwards to China's Xi jiang (West River). Its surface is also broken by closely settled fault-bounded valleys, some with deep lakes. In eastern Yunnan, solution and erosion have transformed extensive surface limestones into a 'forest' of isolated pinnacles (Figure A, page 1). Further east in Guangxi a much larger area of level limestone has been reduced to mountainous remnants (Figure 5.29).

In complete contrast, the Loess Plateau, as its name implies, is covered by great thicknesses of wind-borne dust from central Asia, as is much of the adjacent hill country. Initially grass roots helped to bind the cohesive loess masses, and scrub woodland afforded surface protection; but it is now deeply eroded, and gulleying continues to disrupt the elaborate contoured terracing constructed to exploit its fertility.

China's longest rivers emerge from the western massif through a series of gorges, and respond to a variety of relief features as they flow eastwards. The Huang He, diverted into its great northern loop by the steep edge of the Mongolian borderland, is turned south again by the mountains and cuts

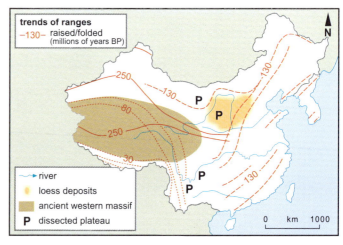

Figure 1.2 Ranges slowly lifted during widely separated geological periods. Though weathered and eroded, they have considerable influence on settlement and communications. The recent, potentially fertile loess deposits, hundreds of metres thick, are prone to gulleying

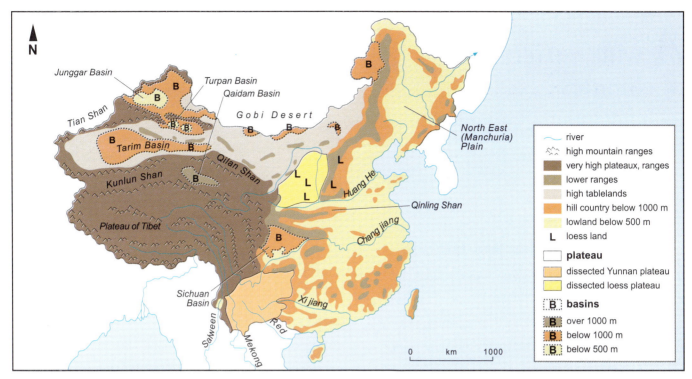

Figure 1.3 Contrasting physical features

into the loess, which provides the load of sediment responsible for its name – the Yellow River. Deflected once more by the Qinling range, it meanders eastward across the North China Plain, its bed built up by deposits, the waters raised dangerously above the fertile countryside.

The Yangtze River acquired high level headwaters by cutting back into the Tibetan plateau. Emerging in its middle course as the Chang jiang (Long River), it receives tributaries from the hilly, mountain-enclosed Sichuan Basin. It then cuts eastwards through spectacular limestone gorges and, with considerable input from the Han, its largest

tributary, breaches the divides between a series of old lake basins before meandering across its wide delta as a navigable outlet to the Pacific.

In the far north east, where the mountain ranges are separated by rolling plains, there is a low divide between two river systems – the Liao draining south and the Songhua north-eastward. Beneath the fertile grasslands lie coal, petroleum, iron ore and other metallic minerals and, of course, along with the physical features and climatic conditions, such resources influence population distribution.

Figure 1.4 Fertile lowlands in Sichuan, where spring is the time for harvesting wheat and rape and transplanting rice seedlings

In Focus ....

● Review the physical processes involved in each of the following statements.

a) China's topography refects its tectonic history, as do the patterns of its large rivers.

b) Over the centuries millions perished as the lower Huang He spilled onto a floodplain, which is now protected by dykes and by upriver control of the water level.

c) The spectacular limestone karst in Guangxi province is a major tourist attraction. A brochure emphasises its green translucent waters – an unusual description for China's rivers, but justified.

A wide variety of climates

Figure 1.6 Early March in northern Shanxi, the fields frozen and unplanted, the trees bare. Notice the numerous chimneys

Influences of location and latitude

In a large country with such contrasts in relief and latitudinal spread there are bound to be considerable climatic variations. Yet the striking differences in mean January temperatures, 16°C in Hainan (18°N) and -19°C at Harbin (46°N), are only partly due to responses to the sun's midday elevation. The seasonal temperatures and precipitation are affected by China's position on the eastern part of an extensive landmass, and therefore by the relative influences of a dry continental interior with a large annual temperature range and an ocean supplying moisture and energy to the air, which seasonally brings in cloud and rain and modifies the temperature. Also, wherever the location within the country, relief and aspect are significant, for steep windward slopes may encourage precipitation yet shelter leeward valleys or basins, and of course, temperature falls with altitude.

Seasonal contrasts

During winter a dense airmass builds over the continental interior and bitterly cold outblowing winds affect western and northern China, frequently carrying dust from the deserts and loess lands. Occasionally, slightly warmer, moister air from the ocean moves into the north east causing snow, though this seldom penetrates far inland.

Towards the south east, winters tend to be milder and cloudier, though occasional eastward surges of cold air conflict with the warmer air, bringing spells of cold, wet or snowy weather to parts of southern China. Figure 1.7 shows that at times the persistent dry, cold north-westerlies may pick up moisture and affect the south east. By contrast some inland basins, such as the fertile Sichuan lowlands, benefit from the compression of subsiding air and are warmer than one might expect.

Figure 1.5 Notice the annual range in mean monthly air temperature and seasonal contrasts in the trends of the isotherms

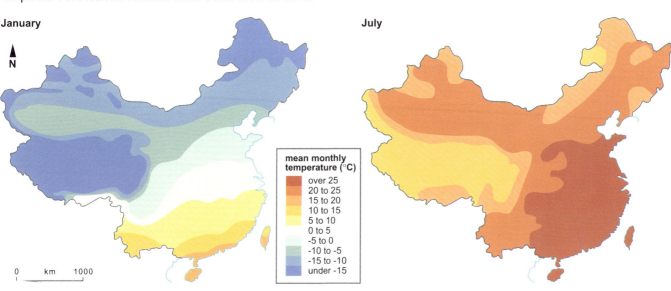

January

July

mean monthly
temperature (°C)

over 25
20 to 25
15 to 20
10 to 15
5 to 10
0 to 5
-5 to 0
-10 to -5
-15 to -10
under -15

0   km   1000

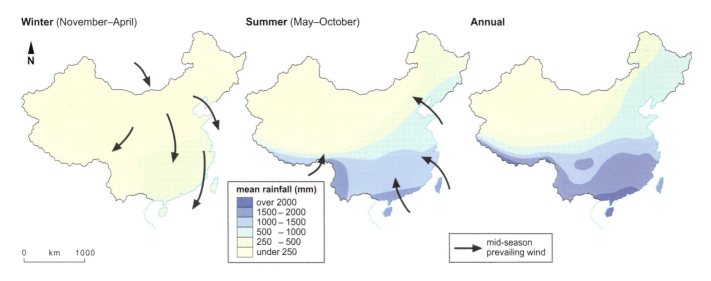

Winter (November–April) **Summer** (May–October) **Annual**

mean rainfall (mm)
- over 2000
- 1500 – 2000
- 1000 – 1500
- 500 – 1000
- 250 – 500
- under 250

→ mid-season prevailing wind

0   km   1000

Figure 1.7 A marked continental effect, with outblowing winter winds and summer monsoonal influence, accounts for the broad rainfall distribution

In summer the continental interior heats up and air pressure falls. A monsoonal inflow sets in from the south east, and occasionally from the south west. By May most of southern China is hot and humid; conditions which extend further north during the following weeks. Rain is not continuous but storms are frequent, with intense downpours when moist airmasses clash with continental air. The south eastern coastlands occasionally experience a **tropical cyclone (typhoon)** moving in from the Pacific with torrential rain and destructive winds. There is variation in duration and extent of the rain from year to year, and eastern central China is sometimes subject to disastrous summer flooding, or an exceptionally dry year.

The country as a whole receives most precipitation during summer. As the moist air moves towards the interior, rainfall tends to diminish with distance from the coast. There are in fact considerable falls on the windward parts of the mountain ranges and high plateaux, which is not apparent in Figure 1.7. Brief, heavy storms affect the loess lands, especially in July, though their occurrence varies from year to year; in fact summer rainfall is particularly unreliable in the drier interior.

Figure 1.5 reflects the effects of altitude on mean air temperature and shows strong latitudinal influences during winter. While Harbin is displaying its renowned ice-sculptures, farmers in the south are harvesting winter wheat and planting a rice crop to follow. In summer there is little difference in mean temperature over much of eastern China, though the daily maximum varies from place to place according to altitude, aspect and cloud cover. In the arid interior the summer midday temperatures are high.

Figure 1.8 Early March in Yunnan, trees in leaf, tall bamboos about the village, and buffaloes ploughing for the second crop, rice

In Focus ....

- Considerable variations in the sun's elevation and the hours with daylight between the northern and southern borders are only partly responsible for the fact that in the eastern provinces there are wider differences in mean air temperatures during winter than there are in summer. Explain this.

- Why, during winter, do many people in northern China mask their lower face when out?

- Explain why south east China, in particular, is likely to experience typhoons during the summer.

Climate and rural activities

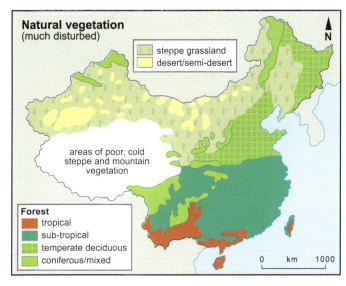

Figure 1.10 Much land is now cultivated (see Figure 1.12), while the grassland becomes semi-arid open steppe towards the west

Influences on natural vegetation

Figure 1.10 indicates the strong climatic influences on the distribution of China's natural vegetation, though this has been greatly modified by settlement. Expanses of sparse scrub cover much of the western tableland, while the mountains are mantled with richer grasses or conifers, according to altitude and aspect. Much of the north west is dry steppe, with salt-tolerant shrubs in desert basins, but valuable areas of pasture grass among the mountains.

To the east the eroded loess lands (Figure 1.3) once bore woody shrubs and grasses, whereas deciduous woodland covered much of the North China Plain, with mixed forest on the adjacent mountains. In the far north east the grasslands still give way to forests of larch and pine.

Areas of forest, varying with altitude but rich in natural resources, also remain in the mountains of western Sichuan and Yunnan. But in the Sichuan Basin continuous rural settlement has cleared most of the red lowland soils of their broad-leaved evergreens, bamboos, occasional palms, and pines, which occur in various associations over much of southern China.

Clearance for cultivation, firewood, and timber has created areas of badland erosion in many parts of the country (Figure 6.24, page 87), though the use of traditional techniques and efficient terracing have produced soil stability over most of rural China.

Influences on rural land use

In Figure 1.12 the thick lines reflect important geographical influences on rural land use, with a north–south boundary between drier pastoral country and moister cultivated lands, and an east–west one between the drier, cooler north, where the main food grains are wheat and millet, and the warmer, moister south, where rice is the main crop. In practice, however, rice is grown in many areas to the north of this and wheat to the south, and other crops are produced before, after or alongside the main grains. Nevertheless the broad divisions are significant.

Figure 1.9 Deciduous fruits, wheat, and maize meticulously inter-bedded in the cold winter regime to the north of Beijing municipality

Figure 1.11 Families working in the rice fields in Sichuan. Winter wheat is stacked in the barns

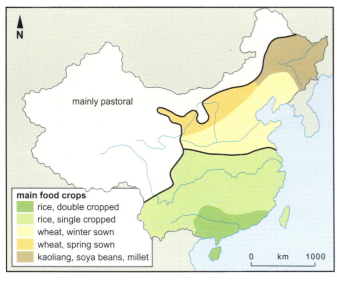

Figure 1.12 In practice there is much regional overlapping of food crops

map legend:

main food crops
- rice, double cropped
- rice, single cropped
- wheat, winter sown
- wheat, spring sown
- kaoliang, soya beans, millet

mainly pastoral

0   km   1000

Figure 1.13 A Dai village in tropical Yunnan, the houses, fencing, and logs reflecting forest clearance

In south east China a winter crop of maize, groundnuts, or fodder gives way to rice, harvested in early summer, followed by a second rice crop – a regime which needs fertilisers and leguminous rotations to maintain yields. Within the south central highlands, in the Sichuan Basin, and on parts of the Yunnan plateau, winter wheat or rape is immediately followed by rice, from a prepared seedbed, with harvesting, flooding and transplanting taking place in a few days. This calls for precise judgement and intensive labour.

On the eastern parts of the North China Plain wheat is planted in autumn, harvested in May, then followed by either sorghum (kaoliang), millet, maize, soya or sweet potatoes. To the west of this, where winters are drier and colder, spring wheat or a hardy millet is sown towards the end of March. Similarly, on the former grasslands of the north east, wheat and maize are grown on a large scale in the southern provinces, whereas further north, with extremely cold winters, it is either spring wheat, millet, sorghum, or soya beans.

The distribution of commercial crops varies with natural conditions, and is also affected by pricing policies and market influences. Cotton is widely cultivated on lowlands in the middle and lower basins of the Huang He and Chang jiang, and in western Shandong, while increasing amounts are grown by irrigation in oases in the far west. Mulberries, associated with silk production, are plentiful in the Sichuan Basin and inland of Shanghai, and oak leaves feed silkworms in Shandong and Liaoning.

Tea is a long-standing crop in the moist hill country in south east and central China, whose mild sub-tropical climate also suits citrus fruits and tree crops which yield vegetable oils, such as tung and camellias. In the tropics there are rubber plantations on Hainan Island and, to a lesser extent, in the far south west; while sugar cane flourishes throughout the moister south, especially on the lowlands of eastern Guangdong.

In the temperate north east, sugar beet is grown on a large scale and a great deal of soya is processed for vegetable oil and used in manufactured foods. However, rape, providing both oil and fibre, is much more widely cultivated, flourishing on the temperate plainlands, in the sheltered western basins and in the tablelands of the south west.

Vegetables are grown intensively throughout rural China, and pigs, chicken, ducks, and fish in local ponds are farmed as sidelines. In recent years, however, favourably located commercial enterprises using modern techniques to grow vegetables have begun to supply huge markets, which distribute produce over a wide area and feed processing plants. In Shandong, for instance, the Shougang vegetable market deals with millions of tonnes of produce a year.

This is necessarily a broad introduction, which ignores, for instance, northern pastoral activities and the ubiquitous banana plants in the south, but demonstrates that there is no such thing as 'typical Chinese agriculture'.

In Focus ....

- Debate the necessity of preserving natural vegetation, bearing in mind the following points.

  a) China is particularly rich in species of plants and vertebrates.

  b) It becomes difficult to feed the increasing population.

  c) Skillful hillside terracing, with minimum soil exposure, checks erosion.

  d) Lumbering now involves partial clearance and replanting before further felling – though there is still illegal deforestation.

  e) Chinese rural landscapes are often visually attractive.

Influences on population distribution

Figure 1.15 A fertile valley west of Chengdu, with typical sturdy, black-tiled houses, intensively farmed, wheat stooked, barns full, flooded terraces with green seedlings beyond the small textile mill

China has a population of 1200 million and, though the rate of increase has been reduced, each year an extra 16 million people add to the pressure on land resources and make it more difficult to find employment and maintain rising living standards.

The stark contrasts in the distribution of population (Figure 1.16) are broadly related to the relief and climate, but are also influenced by the presence of resources and economically attractive locations.

Conditions favouring settled agriculture

From the earliest times the settlement pattern has reflected the potential for settled agriculture. This influence on the overall population distribution remains, for almost 80 per cent of the population is rural, depending directly on farming, related occupations, and activities in small villages and market townships.

Much of western China is high or rugged, with very cold winters and a growing season that is too short for large-scale cultivation. In the arid north west the rural population is concentrated around water sources which can be used to irrigate potentially fertile soils, and also in agricultural settlements associated with the extraction of raw materials for industry or energy generation.

In general most people live in the eastern half of the country, with rural population settled on arable land on floodplains, former lake beds and deltaic flats. There are also concentrations in favourable parts of the loess lands, and in fertile valleys and basins in the highlands. In the north east, however, population distribution is greatly influenced by the location of mineral reserves and the subsequent pull effect of industrial centres.

Urban-industrial concentrations

In productive agricultural regions people tend to concentrate in and about large cities with their adjacent areas of intensive farming. Many of the present industrial cities, like Xian in the loess lands and Luoyang further east, developed as a rural administrative centre serving a rich agricultural countryside, in these cases as dynastic capitals. Today such cities are targeted for industrial development (page 38).

Advantages of location and site can boost urban population, and thus stimulate adjoining activities. For example, the city-ports of Chongqing and Wuhan each flourish where a major tributary joins the Chang jiang. They are both route centres with access to sources of energy and industrial raw materials. At least 3 million people live in each city, with four times as many in the immediate hinterland.

Similar concentrations have built up in the North East, where Liaoning and Jilin provinces have large urban-industrial populations related to an abundance of coal, iron ore, petroleum and other mineral resources, and populous

Figure 1.14 Small houses, with cave dwellings and stores in the eroded loess slopes; the fields beside the frozen river are still bare

Figure 1.16 *(right)* The distribution of 1200 million people in response to climate, relief, soil fertility, available water, natural routeways and technological ability to use resources (which varies over time). The ability of state policies to effect change increases

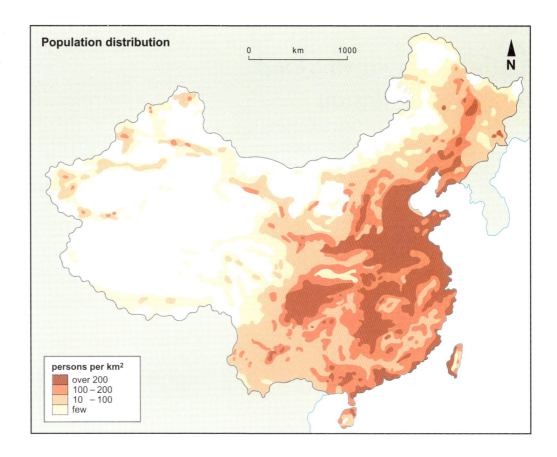

Population distribution

persons per km²
- over 200
- 100 – 200
- 10 – 100
- few

manufacturing cities, like Anshan, Shenyang and Changchun, are supported by many rural communities (page 57).

About Bohai industrial concentrations with available sources of energy and minerals are also supported by local farming. This is a broad economic zone (page 58) which includes the ports of Dalian, Qinhuangdao and Tianjin-Tanggu. Here the capital, Beijing, administers some 30 million people in its metropolitan area.

Coastal concentration

Today China's coastal locations are of particular economic significance. The Government is boosting the development of the eastern coastal fringe, creating **Special Economic Zones** and giving economic privileges for industrial development in and around ports (page 44). There are huge population concentrations about city ports such as Guangzhou, Shanghai and Tianjin, and their influence extends far inland. This is also true of Dalian which serves the north eastern industrial zones, and of the cities about the rim of the Bohai Gulf which have economic links with industrial concentrations in Shandong and Shanxi provinces, and, even those in Shanxi and Nei Mongol.

Shanghai is the focus for an arc of urban-industrial concentration west of the city, and for the 'corridor of economic growth' along the Chang Jiang (page 66), with its

clusters of population about river ports, particularly in Nanjing, Wuhan and Chongqing.

Overall, despite rapid growth in and about inland regional capitals, such as Chengdu in Sichuan and Urumqi in Xinjiang, China's population is concentrated in the east; not simply because of relief and climatic contrasts, but for economic reasons. By boosting eastern coastal zones the Government aims at a spread effect. A proportion of the wealth created will be diverted to poorer interior regions, which have social disadvantages and rapidly growing unemployment. In fact millions migrate from such regions to seek work in the east. Another aim is to use the assets of coastal locations to attract foreign capital to selected ports and industrial areas.

In Focus ....

- Summarise the extent to which factors other than natural conditions are responsible for the distribution of rural and urban population.

- Consider how the pattern might change as rural people, now able to respond to push and pull influences, become more mobile.

Controlling a vast and diverse population

China's population doubled during the first 40 years of The People's Republic, and though the growth rate has fallen (page 46), the 1200 million population poses problems, not simply of size, but of uneven distribution, *ethnic* imbalance, variety of languages and contrasts in living standards and opportunities.

The national minorities

The non-Han peoples number almost 100 million. Official minorities have been exempt from policies aimed at controlling the birth rate. Most live in the less densely populated parts of China, which make up over half the country, and many occupy strategic frontier territory – one reason why increasing numbers of Han Chinese have been settled there. In the north, some 4 million Mongols strive to maintain their own language, script and adherence to Buddism. In the far north west there are about 10 million Turkic-speaking Moslems – Uyghur, Kazakhs, Kirghiz and smaller communities; while about 4 million Tibetan-Burmese speakers live amid the western mountains and high tablelands.

In the south west numerous small groups with strong animist beliefs live among the mountains and river valleys in Sichuan, Yunnan and Guizhou provinces, where several million of the Yi and Mao peoples form scattered clans. There are some 16 million Dai (Thai) speakers in the mountainous south west, the largest group being the Zhuang in Guangxi AR, though there are colourful Dai societies in Yunnan (Figure 1.17) and in parts of Guangdong.

The official Chinese language is Putonghua, based on the northern dialect, Mandarin; but in southern China, and hence in South East Asia, most Chinese, speak Yue (Cantonese).

Social contrasts

Nearly 80 per cent of the population is rural, though there are striking contrasts in living standards and opportunities between the regions with economic potential, earmarked for special development, and the rest. Cities with modern manufacturing and a growth in tertiary activities, attract growing numbers of rural unemployed. Local towns have limited employment opportunities and intensive farming near the cities draws hopeful labourers from less developed or over-populated parts of the hinterland. Such migration has become difficult to control.

The One-Child-Only policy

Population control has become a priority. A one-child-per-family policy was introduced in the 1970s, encouraging late marriage and family planning and emphasising the likely effects of increasing population on living standards. Compliance has meant extra allowances, preferential medical treatment, housing priorities and other benefits. Ethnic minorities have been exempt from such constraints, though, as their numbers have soared, forms of control are now being advocated.

Figure 1.17 Mothers and children in a Dai village in the tropical south west

Figure 1.18 A 'One-Child-Only' poster in Chengdu, with the emphasis on a girl

Figure 1.19 People in Guangzhou, with different purposes, styles and language from those in the Dai village in Figure 1.17

Population growth and distribution

Over the years the policy has become more flexible; partly to counter improper coercion by over-zealous local officials, partly in response to cases of female infanticide, but mainly to acknowledge the advantages of extra labour for farming families and their wish for family support in old age, by allowing a second child if the first were a girl.

The overall policy remains, though it is changing the structure of Chinese society in a number of ways. Its implementation has been harshly portrayed by some foreign media, but within a generation the birth rate fell from 21 per thousand to 12 per thousand. It is in the universal, as well as the national interest, to stabilise a population which is nearly one-quarter of the human race. Successful family planning is closely linked to standards of living and education, and the provision of a welfare system to care for the elderly. The birth rate has fallen particularly rapidly in the large urban areas where such amenities are more readily available. For the future, however, China is faced with an ageing population and the social consequences of a generation with few family ties – no cousins, aunts, or uncles.

Despite the huge population increase, overall living conditions are immeasurably better than they were when The People's Republic came into being. The average life span is now some 70 years, compared with 35 years in 1949, when 80 per cent of the population could neither read nor write (compared with 85 per cent literacy today). Nevertheless, about 180 million Chinese are still illiterate or semi-literate, and some 80 million, mainly in the more mountainous western regions, still struggle to avoid poverty. Financial inputs and specialist aid for backward parts of the country will largely depend on wealth created in the more prosperous East – part of the spread effect.

Figures 1.20 and 1.21 Rural contrast: brother and sister, well-dressed and confident, carrying vegetables and sugar-cane, lunch at a Jinghong market stall. A hill villager, cheerful despite obvious poverty, arrives at Puxiong, a small town in the western mountains

In Focus ....

- Explain why, generally, better standards of living and educational and cultural opportunities tend to bring down the birth rate, and why population control must involve improving conditions for people in the poorer parts of China.

- Why has the structure of four grandparents, two parents and one child been called the '4:2:1 social malady'? Look at the consequent side-effects, such as fear of retirement and the 'little emperor' (spoilt child).

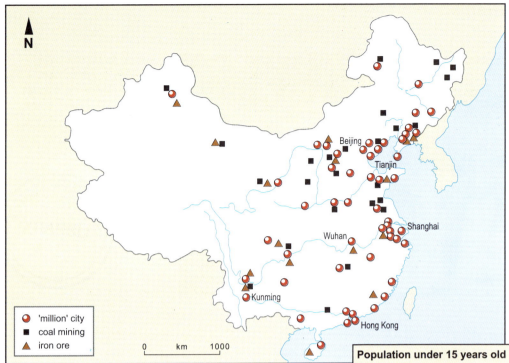

Figure 1.22 *(left)* The distribution of 'million' cities, and large-scale mining of coal (Figure 4.5) and iron ore

Figure 1.23 *(below)* A pattern partly reflecting social-economic conditions at the provincial level, and suggesting consequences for the next generation occupying the eastern provinces and the Autonomous Regions (page 4)

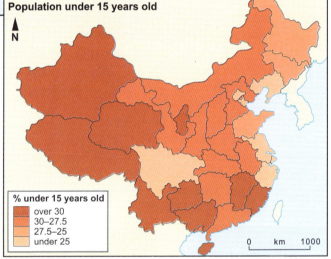

Population under 15 years old

% under 15 years old
over 30
30–27.5
27.5–25
under 25

Notice how Sichuan, in the interior but nevertheless the most populous province, has successfully maintained a low *fertility* level. This province has attracted settlers through the ages and has in fact initiated many of China's successful social policies.

To examine past influences on population size, a pyramid, with information from the 1990 Census, is included on page 46. This demonstrates the overall success of the one-child policy in reducing the rate of increase, although it indicates a relaxation of the policy in recent years.

In Focus ....

- Look at Figures 1.16 (page 13) and 1.22 and consider the relative influences on the present population distribution of natural conditions, of the location of sources of energy and minerals for manufacturing, and of places with potential for industrial development or for commerce.

- Assess the factors which most affected population distribution before the nineteenth century.

- Comment on the statement that 'the influence of natural features on population distribution tends to decline with economic growth'.

- Explain the fact that the relationship between the development of communications and concentrations of population is mutual, one acting to affect the other.

- Regionally the density of population is not only affected by physical and economic factors but by the social customs and behaviour of individual communities. Examine how this is illustrated by the variations in density among China's Provinces and Autonomous Regions.

- Figure 1.23 shows the high levels of fertility and relatively low levels of mortality in areas with large numbers of ethnic minorities, exempt from the one-child policy. There are now moves to tighten population control in these regions. Consider the consequences of the present high population of under 15 year-olds for the future population density of these parts of the country.

- Suggest why there is low fertility and low mortality in the demographically more mature provinces, especially in those with a coastline, where less than 25 per cent of the population is under 15 years old.

From Empire to Republic

PART 2

Separate states to expanding Empire

China's cultural heritage is reflected in the country's way of life, where the social structure has been maintained, with modifications, for over 2000 years. During that time remarkable innovations have affected contemporary society – the concepts of philosophers, early medical knowledge, and the achievements of engineers, craftsmen and artists, and their influences have persisted. Many innovations in China were far in advance of those in comparable civilisations, among them the brush-pen and paper, grid mapping, cast iron, magnetic compasses, seismographic earthquake detection, and deep drilling for brine and natural gas. For thousands of years farming families passed down and retained practical ways of doing things, for example the method of terracing land, constructing kilns and building walls. Though change is accelerating, China is still largely rural, and scenes familiar from age-old paintings and pottery are apparent on any journey though the country.

Figure 2.1 The Great Wall, much restored under the Ming, winds along steep ridges in the Yanshan. Eastern sections are now renovated for the valuable tourist industry

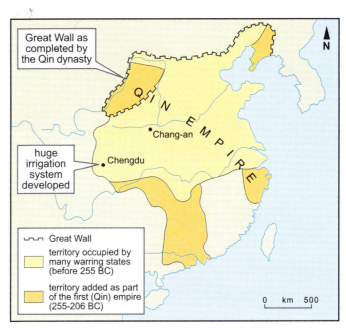

Great Wall as completed by the Qin dynasty

huge irrigation system developed

Chang-an

Chengdu

QIN EMPIRE

N

Great Wall

territory occupied by many warring states (before 255 BC)

territory added as part of the first (Qin) empire (255-206 BC)

0   km   500

Figure 2.2 The Qin Empire embraced states which had a long history of cultured society and significant practical achievements

Developing a structured society

Families were farming river valleys and plains some 7000 years ago. In about 1700 BC, tribal groups came together under a single ruler, signalling the start of the Shang dynasty centred about the lower Huang He, which lasted some 600 years. They were succeeded by a former nomadic people, the Zhou, who over the centuries struggled to control other increasingly independent, feuding states, many protected by walls. During this period societies became remarkably sophisticated. Noble families lived in considerable luxury, officials communicated through pictograph writing and communities included skilled potters and metal workers.

During the sixth century Confucius (Kungzi) wandered between states, propounding the concept of a structured society with understanding rulers, loyal subjects, honest scholars, and youth respectful of elders. In fact strong family life, with reverence for ancestors, was already a part of Chinese society. The acceptance of a **Confucian** society in which individuals acknowledged their role, from the common people, through ranks of officials, to the emperor, made for successful administration throughout imperial times.

A century before Confucius, the scholar Lao Zi and others had considered how people, as a part of nature, might adopt a Way (Dao) of living in harmony with their environment. Over the ages, **Daoism**, sometimes linked with Buddhism, enabled people to look for natural harmony, and come to terms with waywardness in nature and society without the trappings of an orthodox religion.

Figure 2.3 An outline of imperial expansion under the Han, and the development of trading activities, with movement along routes which brought commercial gains and introduced Buddhism

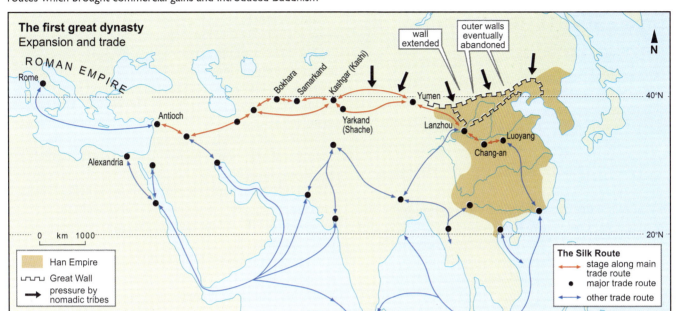

'Empire' with autocracy

In 256 BC fighting among the states ended the Zhou dynasty, and the Qin, occupying loess land about Chang-an (Xian), became dominant. In 221 BC their ruler, Shi Huang Di, established a unified 'empire'. Central control through civilian and military governors enabled him to standardise writing, coinage, weights and measures and even cart axles, which meant all wheels would fit ruts throughout the states.

As with many strong rulers, ruthlessness led to exploitation and persecution. Shi Huang Di aimed to destroy former ruling families and the influence of Confucian scholars, burning much of their literature. Forced labour, involving hundreds of thousands, was used to link and extend state walls, providing a barrier, the **Great Wall**, which eventually stretched 2500 km from north-western borderlands to the sea. Potters toiled to create a vast terracotta army to accompany Shi Huang Di to the next world, which is still being excavated about Xian. His death in 210 BC brought vengeful uprising which, four years later, ushered in the Empire's first great dynasty – the **Han**. In his brief reign Shi Huang Di had re-established a *bureaucratic* control, through which the Han could, and did, create a lasting social structure.

Empire prospers under the Han

The Han dynasties controlled an expanding empire for more than four centuries, first from Xian, then, after a brief usurpation (AD 9–24), from Luoyang. They extended control southward, with garrisons in Sichuan and far beyond the Xi River. Traders carried silk along routes north of the Tibetan plateau, through Afghanistan and Persia to the Mediterranean and Rome, and in return brought gold, silver and precious stones. Hundreds of years later pack animals maintained a flow of commodities from merchant to merchant along this **Silk Route** (Figure 2.3).

Agriculture flourished with the aid of iron implements, fertilisers, seed drills, water mills and intricate irrigation systems based on major canal projects. Farmers benefited, though at times they were burdened by taxation. Confucian principles were re-adopted, and a scholar-official class virtually formed an active civil service. As the state expanded and prospered, so did art and fine craftsmanship. Today most Chinese acknowledge this flourishing empire by regarding themselves as 'Han'.

When the second Han dynasty broke down in 220 AD, various kingdoms fought for supremacy. Tartars from central Asia, the Wei, effectively controlled the north and maintained advances in cultivation and irrigation. They also spread Buddhism, introduced from India during the first century AD, establishing monasteries, temples and pagodas.

In Focus ....

● The Han flourished during this remarkable period, with the Roman Empire at its height, Christianity being established, Buddhism spreading, and China adopting an administration based on Confucian principles. Consider how, beside the practical innovations listed above, such distant events have continued to affect the structure and distribution of languages, legal systems and religions over the ages.

The Empire absorbs its conquerors

With the fall of the Han much of China remained turbulent, until in 581 AD the Sui, also from the north west, re-unified the country. They linked the north with the increasingly prosperous rice lands by using a massive labour force to create a waterway between the Chang jiang and Huang He – the Grand Canal (page 80). When unrest, partly related to forced labour, brought the Sui down, it led to the Tang succession, which was to make China one of the world's most powerful states.

Five hundred innovative years

The period of the Tang Dynasty, AD 618 to 907, has been called a 'Golden Age'. China was the world's largest state, with a population of over 70 million organised by an educated civil service. One million people lived in the capital, Chang-an. Block-printing now allowed textbooks and scrolls to be widely distributed, an aid to administration and culture. Poets and painters produced beautiful, lasting works, and potters crafted translucent porcelains, their superb Tang horses reflecting trade with the West. Commerce flourished internally, between the northern walled cities and the now populous central southern parts of China which supplied increasing amounts of rice. This enabled southern cities to prosper – Hangzhou's suburbs were enclosed by a 40 km long wall.

The collapse of the dynasty in AD 907 led to new invasions from the north east. Yet by AD 940 the Song dynasty was established at Kaifeng, and cultural and technological progress continued. The nobility were patrons of art and science, while the printing presses disseminated education more widely. There were innovations in flood control and irrigation, with fish-farming in village ponds and flooded rice fields, which also reduced mosquito larvae. The wealth of landlords increased, while the bulk of the population enjoyed low taxation. Unfortunately, the increasing use of iron for implements, nails, weapons and coins, requiring charcoal, depleted the northern forests.

Despite, or because of, such achievements, in 1127 increasing threats from nomadic tribes forced the Song to move their capital south to Hangzhou. Early in the thirteenth century Genghis Khan invaded, and by 1223 the Mongols controlled China north of the Huang He. Yet, once again, the bureaucratic chain survived. In 1271 Kublai Khan, grandson of Genghis, relying on an experienced civil service, proclaimed himself Emperor, and after removing the southern Song brought the whole country under the rule of his Yuan dynasty.

As China was part of a wider Mongol control, extending to Persia and eastern Europe, trade along the Silk Route increased. Merchants also introduced the Islamic and Christian faiths – this was the time of Marco Polo's sojourn in China. The prestige of China was high and it passed on its knowledge of printing techniques and gunpowder, along with other merchandise, to the West.

A new capital – Dadu (Great City), also known as Khanbalik – was constructed where Beijing now stands. The

Figure 2.4 The tomb of the third Tang Emperor and his wife, the Empress Wu, dominates the loess landscape near Xian, with contoured terraces on the slopes. Houses with storerooms in caves border the deep gulley; others shelter in the pits in the foreground. To the left is the statue-flanked approach

Figure 2.5 *(right)* The extraordinary extent of Mongol control over Asia and eastern Europe allowed the Empire to expand under the Yuan; yet in China their domination was relatively brief

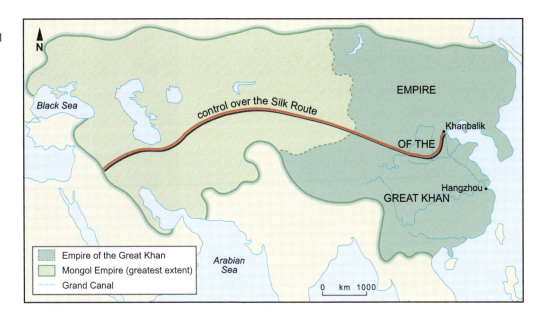

Grand Canal was re-routed and with the use of lock-gates, extended to serve the capital. But after the death of Kublai Khan, Mongol leadership weakened. In a sense the Chinese had absorbed the conquerors. In 1352 an over-taxed peasantry ended Mongol rule.

Restoration, innovation, isolation

The Ming established their court at Nanjing. However, with a vulnerable northern frontier the Third Emperor moved the capital to Beijing, and widened eastern parts of the Great Wall for troop movements. Recalling the 'golden age' of the Tang and Song, they stressed Confucian ideals, renovated historic sites, and created their own distinctive architectural styles. The Court, the powerful, and the rich maintained considerable grandeur, encouraging literature and art, and craftsmen produced superb articles of porcelain, ceramic

and cloisonée. Among practical advances in agriculture, quick-growing rice strains allowed double-cropping in the south.

In an era of prosperity, the population almost doubled to 150 million, yet this extra pressure on the land meant that peasant producers gained relatively little and there was much rural poverty. The Court, who had created the Forbidden City and Temple of Heaven, became increasingly isolated, observing intricate rituals. Appointing scholar-administrators by examination favoured those with land and rank, who maintained control while scorning the prospering merchants. Class divisions remained sharp, for peasants also distrusted merchants, who bought goods at low prices and made a profit.

In 1644 a combination of treachery, rebellion, and invasion ended the Ming dynasty. Corruption surrounded the Emperor, there were famines and uprising in the north west, and a powerful tribal alliance, the Manchu, invaded from the north east.

Figure 2.6 *(above)* The Nine-Dragon Screen through an archway in the lavish Forbidden City which was established by the third Ming Emperor

In Focus ....

- Consider why the following are as relevant to the period described as they are now.

  a) The need to transport commodities, food in particular, makes for technological improvements in transport and communications.

  b) Useful technological innovations are often accompanied by environmental degradation.

  c) Economic growth at the national level does not necessarily improve living standards throughout society.

Foreign impacts: the fall of Empire

Retreat into isolation

In the early days of their new Qing dynasty, the Manchu expanded their empire north eastwards to the Heilong jiang (Amur River) and north westward towards the growing Russian empire. Until the mid-eighteenth century capable Qing rulers achieved a degree of stability. Chinese culture had again absorbed its conquerors, but the Court was becoming increasingly inward-looking, involved with customs and ritual. Stability had brought a sense of power which justified, to them at least, a policy of self-sufficiency. In reality they were isolating the nation from the scientific and commercial expansion taking place in Western countries. As foreign intruders, appointing Manchu officials, they were in any case distanced from the people. It was this society that the West was to breach.

Opium war and peasant rebellion

Portugal had had a trading base at Macao since 1557, and European nations were anxious to trade with China. During the eighteenth century their ships visited ports in the south east, especially Guangzhou (Canton). The Qing, however, were opposed to trading with the West, and in 1757

Figure 2.7 Hong Kong has come to rely on the mainland for water piped through the New Territories, and also for energy resources and fresh food

Figure 2.8 Shamian island in Guangzhou became a British and French concession. Most of their residences, like this French colonial building, are now flats or offices

stipulated that foreign trade must pass through 'factories' (compounds of local landlords) near Guangzhou.

The British, who originally traded tea, silk and ceramics in exchange for silver, began to trade opium from Bengal, draining huge amounts of silver from China. In 1800 the Emperor banned its import, though the British in particular persisted. In 1839 Chinese officials burnt merchants' stock and attempted to blockade foreign vessels in the Pearl River. Defeated in the subsequent Opium War of 1840-2, China was forced to negotiate the Treaty of Nanking, yielding Hong Kong island to Britain and granting the right to trade through **treaty ports** – rights extended to France, USA, Italy and Germany.

China's peasant population, beset by land shortage and high taxes, was desperately poor, and deeply resented Manchu rule. From 1850 rebellion in southern China spread rapidly, and for 15 years people fought to remove Manchu domination. The Taiping Rebellion demonstrated the peasant's power, but there was a high price to pay – some 20 million perished.

Europeans exact 'rights'

Europeans were involved in many skirmishes during the rebellion. In 1856 the British forced a weakening Manchu Government to concede more trading rights and to legalise the opium trade. In 1860 the Emperor fled Beijing, and British and French troops sacked the Summer Palace. But in 1864, fearing success by an increasingly unpredictable rebellious faction, European powers helped the Manchu to enforce surrender. In return they gained trading areas, over

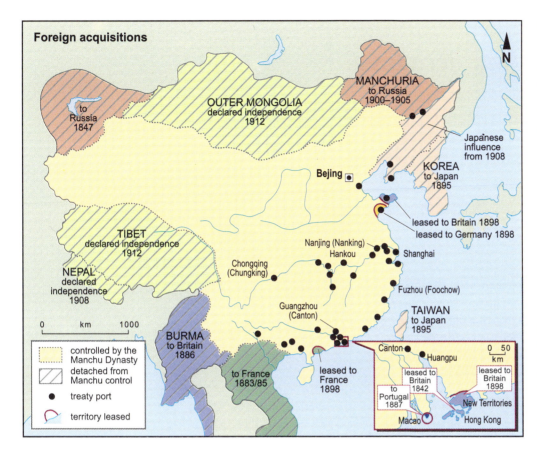

Foreign acquisitions

MANCHURIA
to Russia
1900–1905

OUTER MONGOLIA
declared independence
1912

to
Russia
1847

Japanese
influence
from 1908

Bejing

KOREA
to Japan
1895

leased to Britain 1898
leased to Germany 1898

TIBET
declared independence
1912

NEPAL
declared
independence
1908

Nanjing (Nanking)
Hankou

Chongqing
(Chungking)

Shanghai

Fuzhou (Foochow)

Guangzhou
(Canton)

TAIWAN
to Japan
1895

0   km   1000

BURMA
to Britain
1886

to France
1883/85

leased to
France
1898

Canton

Huangpu

0   50
km

leased to
Britain
1842

leased to
Britain
1898

to
Portugal
1887

New Territories

Macao

Hong Kong

controlled by the
Manchu Dynasty

detached from
Manchu control

treaty port

territory leased

Figure 2.9 Foreign acquisitions – Notice the spread of the treaty ports up the Chang and Xi Rivers and their tributaries, increasing the commercial significance of Shanghai, Guangzhou, and Hong Kong

Figure 2.10 (below) Occupied territory rapidly came to acquire foreign characteristics. Hong Kong, with sturdy banks, business houses, and trams retains British characteristics, while acquiring high-rise anonymity (page 76)

which each nation had special influence. In 1861 Britain had acquired Kowloon peninsula, and in 1898 obtained the New Territories of Hong Kong on a 99-year lease (page 76). In 1885 China's tributary state, Vietnam, had gone to France, in 1886 Britain took upper Burma, while in 1895 Japan disabled the Chinese fleet and seized Taiwan and other islands, leaving Korea nominally independent.

The end of Empire

Within China there was, naturally, much anti-foreign feeling. In 1901 the old Dowager Empress Ci-Xi, the power behind the throne since 1861, allowed troops to back up a 55-day siege of foreign legations in Beijing, started by an anti-foreign Society known as 'The Boxers'. Following relief by an international force, foreign powers took an even firmer grip on the country, not only by military presence but economically through the operation of banks, shipping, insurance, railways and trading companies. They maintained absolute control in concession areas and around the treaty ports, many of them far inland.

When the Dowager Empress died in 1908 the powerless Emperor was killed by intrigue, leaving a two year-old nephew, Pu-Yi as the last Emperor. In 1911 a Revolutionary Alliance seized control, and the Manchu dynasty ended with the proclamation of **The Chinese Republic** in January 1912.

In Focus ....

- Examine the combination of circumstances which made it possible for European powers to dominate such a large, though divided, nation.

- Why did Manchu domination over such a brief period in Chinese history so severely set back a nation with a long record of technical innovations and cultural achievements?

23

The Republic: four decades of exploitation

The turbulent 1920s

The Chinese Republic was proclaimed by Sun Yat-sen, who had long worked for revolution. Yet he was soon replaced as President by a warlord anxious to become Emperor, but who died in 1916. Nevertheless other regional warlords controlled their own armies and levied local taxes, and Sun Yat-sen's Nationalist Revolutionary Party (*Guomindang*) was banned.

During the 1914-18 War China, an ally of Britain, France and the USA, allowed Japan to remove the Germans from Shandong; though when Japan remained there and demanded control over mineral-rich Manchuria, China's former allies remained passive.

In 1921 the **Chinese Communist Party** (CCP) held its first Congress, backed by Russia, who also supported the Nationalists, seeking a joint force able to oust the warlords and their 'ragged armies'. The CCP recruited widely among peasants, and in 1926 joined Nationalist forces in southern China under Chiang Kai-shek, who had succeeded Sun Yat-sen. They marched north as separate armies, and by March 1927 the CCP had taken Wuhan and the Nationalists had entered Shanghai, where British troops guarded foreign concessions. But suddenly Chiang Kai-shek turned on the Communists, driving them south into the rugged eastern hills, and in January 1928 he proclaimed Nanjing capital of **The Nationalist Republic of China** before marching north to take Beijing.

Nationalist attempts to wipe out the Communists were diverted in 1931 by Japan's invasion of Manchuria. Japanese air and naval attacks on Shanghai forced Chiang Kai-shek to recognise Manchuria as a separate state, ruled by Pu-Yi, under Japan's control.

The Long March

In June 1935 some 100 000 Communists, driven from the eastern hills, fought their way westward as a Red Army under Mao Zedong, Chairman of the CCP, battling across

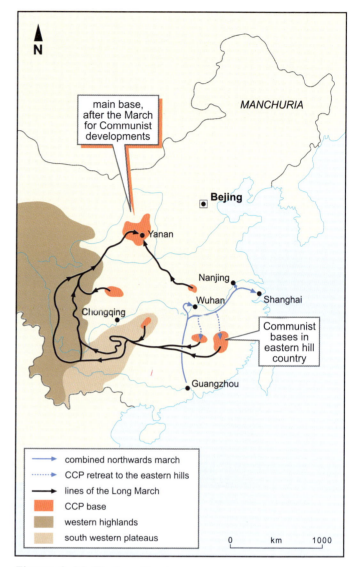

Figure 2.11 The Long March

the Chang jiang into the western mountains, then northward, suffering great casualties. Leaving the snow-covered mountains, they eventually reached Yanan in Shaanxi province after a 'march' of 358 days. There in the loess lands 20 000 survivors, many settled in hillside caves, developed the Communist heartland. To the Chinese **The Long March** is an epic story of courage which foreshadowed the rise of The People's Republic.

Meanwhile, as the Nationalists sought foreign aid to reconstruct and provide armaments, the watching Japanese were poised to attack. Mao, organising Communist communities about Yanan, had already declared war on Japan, but realised that the Chinese would have to act together. In fact pro-Communist troops trapped the Nationalist leader, Chiang Kai-shek, near Xian, and held him until he agreed to co-operate. When Japan invaded in 1937 in theory they faced a United Front.

The Japanese invasion

Forced to abandon first Shanghai and then Nanjing, the Chinese moved their capital to Chongqing, leaving the Japanese to control the area shown in Figure 2.12, though undertaking guerilla warfare within it. China received military supplies from the former USSR, European nations, and the USA, although diplomatically this was an 'incident' and not 'war'.

During the 1939-45 War it was difficult to supply China. The Russians were besieged and Japan had cut the Burma Road to Kunming, though transport planes reached western

Figure 2.13 *(above)* Decisive battles were fought along this Dadu gorge as the Communists followed river routes northwards

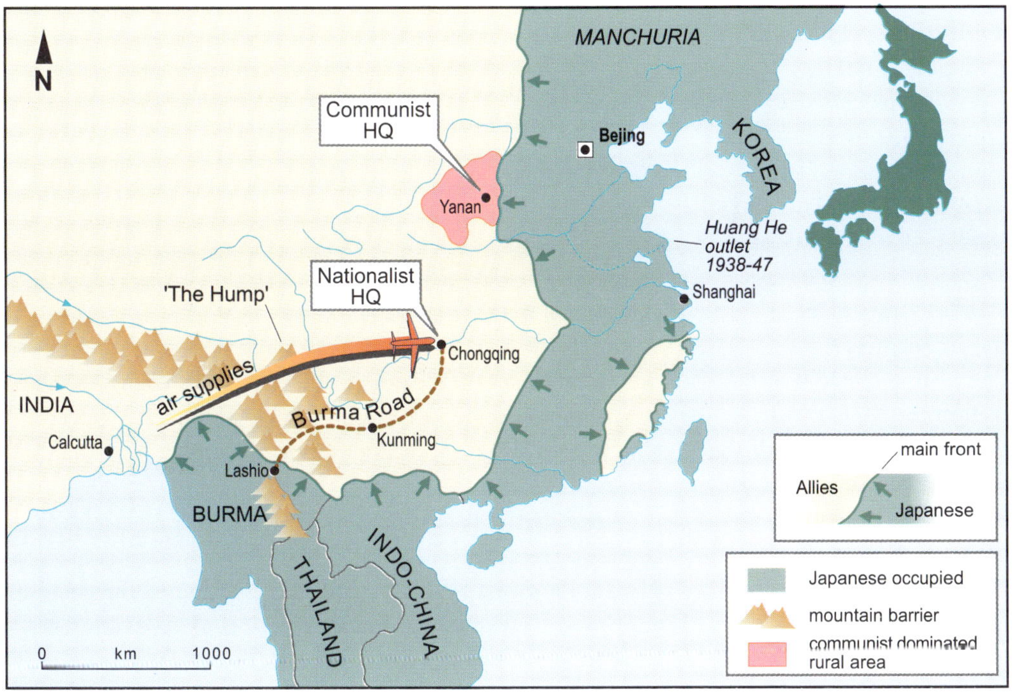

Figure 2.12 The area of maximum Japanese occupation, within which Chinese waged guerilla warfare. From 1942 Allied armies confronted Japan in southern Asia; with the Burma Road cut, they sent supplies to China from airfields constructed in north east India

China from north east India. Unfortunately, the United Front meant little. In the north the Communists fought large-scale guerilla actions, continuing to reform peasant societies, while many Nationalists regarded the war as an interruption to their campaign against the Communists.

Defeat for the nationalists

In 1945 the atomic bombs suddenly ended the war with Japan. The Communists, receiving surrendered arms and ammunition, made for vital industrial centres in Manchuria, where the USSR had belatedly confronted the Japanese. The Nationalists also rushed north. All out civil war began in 1947, ending with the general advance of the Red Army, renamed The People's Liberation Army (PLA). As they advanced, the CCP introduced land reforms, winning the support of local peasantry and building up trust for Mao and his followers. The Nationalists' defeat was hastened by

corruption in their midst and by inflation which had ruined many business supporters.

In October 1949 Mao Zedong announced the creation of **The People's Republic of China** (PRC), with government once more located in Beijing. Chiang Kai-shek moved to Taiwan, liberated from the Japanese, and early in 1950 the last of his forces fled from Hainan to join Nationalist China – officially the Taiwanese Republic of China (page 78).

In Focus ....

● Consider why the heroism involved in the events of the Great March and opposition to Japan gave The People's Republic such an impetus, and, in later years, made for such loyalty to Mao Zedong, despite his errors of judgement (page 27).

Social reorganisation: successes and failures

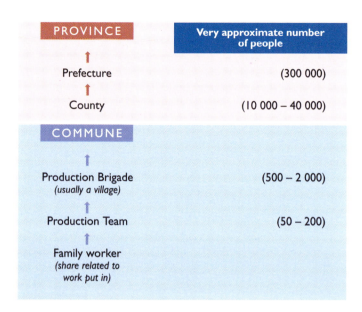

PROVINCE	Very approximate number of people
↑	
Prefecture	(300 000)
↑	
County	(10 000 – 40 000)
COMMUNE	
↑	
Production Brigade *(usually a village)*	(500 – 2 000)
↑	
Production Team	(50 – 200)
↑	
Family worker *(share related to work put in)*	

Figure 2.15 The Commune system

The People's Republic faced great difficulties. China was shattered by years of fighting and 80 per cent of its population was illiterate. Foreign powers had given up Chinese territory, except for British Hong Kong and Portuguese Macao, and most foreign firms and banks had withdrawn, suspicious of the new regime. It was essential to replace war-damaged industries, and in 1950 a Treaty of Friendship and Alliance with the USSR allowed the Russians to provide loans, equipment and technicians so that factories could produce machinery for engineering, agriculture, mines and vehicles, and also to manufacture armaments, as the PLA was engaged in the Korean War during 1950-3. The Government had to balance agricultural and industrial development, for agriculture had to feed an impoverished nation and, as one of the few sources of national income, produce for export.

The people's communes

The People's Republic dispossessed most landlords and redistributed their land among peasant families, but it was soon clear that uneducated farmers working small plots was

Figure 2.14 Part of a village team in Yunnan, working together to replant rice seedlings from the bed in the foreground

an inefficient way of increasing production, especially with a shortage of machinery and transport. In the countryside voluntary *co-operatives* were set up – with people pooling their land, marketing through the state and sharing income according to their contributions. Large co-operatives were able to gain sufficient capital to buy machinery and establish light industries.

However, the Party felt that the whole way of rural life should be reorganised. In 1958 Mao Zedong announced plans for a 'Great Leap Forward' and established the chain of administration shown in Figure 2.15. People's communes were set up to manage agriculture, light industries and local administration, and to give their brigades (mostly villages) quotas for the commodities that their teams should produce. In addition each village family could farm a small allotment. Also the communes could be combined for large projects, such as constructing irrigation canals or water storages. This proved a wise decision, bringing real benefits. There were variations, but until the late 1970s communes were the foundation of rural life over most of China – although right for that time, however they later inhibited plans to expand production (page 28).

Setbacks during the 1960s

Other facets of the Great Leap Forward proved less successful. Attempts to spread manufacturing by setting up local iron and steel furnaces proved disastrous – failing to produce quality products, disrupting rural life and denuding local woodland. In the early 1960s other major setbacks occurred. Climatic conditions led to failed harvests and subsequent famines, with great loss of life. Then as China and the USSR disagreed over principles, Russia withdrew all aid and technicians. As most of the export earnings came from agricultural produce and coal, China could only afford to import absolute essentials from those willing to trade. There was a struggle to maintain industrial development, even without the political chaos which was to follow.

The effects of the Cultural Revolution

In the Communist Party there was strife over principles. Mao Zedong, still conscious of public adulation, assumed a dictatorial role. Capable scientists, engineers, managers and academics were portrayed as an unacceptable privileged class and their use of foreign techniques denounced as 'undesirable Western influence'. In 1966 Mao initiated the Cultural Revolution, enlisting millions of young people as Red Guards to act against those who showed 'bourgeois beliefs'. Many liberal thinkers, politicians, scientists, teachers and students were imprisoned or sent to labour in the countryside. Minorities suffered, religious buildings were closed and actions against foreigners severed contacts which might have aided modernisation. After four years of violence the Red Guards were disbanded. Yet Mao retained the respect of the masses, partly through self-promotion, but mainly in view of past achievements.

In Focus ....

- Consider how this period under Mao illustrates the advantages and disadvantages of control by a Party that was able to mobilise millions for practical projects but one also able to quash opposition.

- Apart from the fiasco of focusing on local steel production, attempts to increase grain yields involved the mass destruction of small birds. The result was crop devastation by other lifeforms. Suggest why this should have been obvious, yet still went ahead.

During the 1970s, after the American withdrawal from Vietnam, direct contacts with the USA, Japan and European countries increased. In 1971 The People's Republic was admitted as a member of the United Nations, though the USA did not fully recognise the PRC until 1979. Strategic *hi-tech* developments had been given priority and in 1975 China, now a nuclear power, launched and recovered a space satellite.

When Mao Zedong died in 1976 a struggle for power led to the arrest of his widow and her associates known as the 'Gang of Four', and to control by those favouring modernisation and contacts with the West. They were to introduce a 'socialist market economy system' and over the next two decades established new trade links, made use of foreign expertise and investment in enterprises, and sought overseas funding for projects aimed at economic growth.

Figure 2.16 Wall-building by a team tamping loess earth between adjustable shuttering, a process unchanged through the centuries – in fact the method by which the Great Wall was constructed, prior to facing

Figure 2.17 *(right)* A concrete canal and reservoir, built by a labour force from various communes, and part of a system irrigating the countryside north of Xian. The replacement of the commune system by individual and collective responsibility groups has made such projects more difficult to implement. Today it means funding contract work

The move to a market economy

Shortage of skill and lack of incentive

In the immediate post-Mao years, China faced the aftermath of the Cultural Revolution. The shortage of scientists, academics and those skilled in management made it difficult to train sufficient technicians to resuscitate stagnant industries. Many politicians opposed to Mao had suffered and the country was burdened with a commune system which had done much for the people, yet had led to stagnation and economic disasters.

The State Planning Organisation (SPO) required each commune to produce a certain quantity of a commodity (a quota) at a fixed price. The commune then established quotas for its brigades (Figure 2.15, page 26), whose local administrators (*cadres*) organised production teams of 20 or so families. All shared the profits from the quota and from the sale of any surplus. Unfortunately, local conditions did not always suit state requirements; for instance wheat might be grown to meet a quota when another crop would have been more suitable.

Figure 2.19 Lagoons created beside Lake Dian are backed by farmland running back to fault-bounded ranges near Kunming. They are stocked with fish and maintained by family groups, helped by experts (Figure 2.20)

The communes, through the brigades, managed machine maintenance, draught animals, transport, and local processing. They also supervised education, health, welfare and political activities. Yet, overall, the teams nominally in charge of production and the members receiving their share had little incentive to realise the full potential of the land. Nationally, low productivity was failing to meet the needs of a rapidly growing population.

The same situation has affected state-controlled industries, whose factories have often carried an excess

Figure 2.18 A family group farming leased holdings on the Min lowlands – here removing the last of the wheat harvest and ploughing stubble beside prepared seedbeds and flooded fields. The village in the woods beyond has furniture works supplied by a group with an agreed lumber contract

Figure 2.20 *(left)* Experts checking fish populations by samples from the lagoon

Figure 2.21 *(below)* A family group, wire-cutting in a township near Jinghong, provides contract fencing

labour force – workers assured of a job, basic rations, health treatment, and other social benefits, their 'iron rice bowl'. Also, there are few incentives for initiative by a management which has little control over materials, marketing or investing profits. Today state-owned industries find it difficult to be profitable while guaranteeing employment and funding such amenities (page 37), and a great many manufacturing enterprises are now privately controlled.

Encouraging initiative

During the late 1970s more liberal state officials, including Deng Xiaoping, focused attention on the need to combat under-achievement through a policy of **four modernisations** – of agriculture, industry, science and technology.

The commune hierarchy was replaced by administration through committees in local 'administrative townships'. A **responsibility contract system** was introduced under which individuals, families and collective groups could contract to lease land for a specific purpose, or engage in a particular enterprise (page 32). With families rewarded for initiative and skill, family purchasing power has increased and so, therefore, has retail and manufacturing activity in rural towns, where entrepreneurs can set up firms and recruit labour from a wider area. More and more family members not directly involved in farming are setting up small commercial enterprises.

This activity has undoubtedly stimulated productivity and allowed many rural families to prosper, though by no means all. There have been negative effects (page 32). With provinces distributing state subsidies for particular projects there have been loopholes for local profiteers. Because of their know-how, many former commune cadres became local administrators, able to favour the enterprises of associates by allocating state subsidies, enterprises which have not necessarily benefited rural communities. There

have also been disagreements between provinces and central Government over taxes and distribution of subsidies.

Welfare amenities formerly provided under the commune system are not always available, and those that are may have to be paid for. Nor does everyone have the opportunity to profit from initiative, since over-population and a lower demand for labour on the land have resulted in rural unemployment, which is leading to large-scale rural-urban migration (page 33). Also removing subsidies, which for so long rigidly controlled prices, has led to inflation, experienced for the first time by millions, with considerable dissatisfaction.

However, despite the disadvantages, the introduction of a socialist market economy system has enabled many rural communities and townships to prosper, and with the encouragement of foreign participation in manufacturing enterprises and capital projects there has been spectacular growth of the national economy. The impact of these policies on rural and urban communities are considered further in Parts 3-6, as are contrasts in development between various parts of China.

In Focus ....

- The increase in sideline activities and semi-skilled work enables rural communities to afford to buy more consumer goods in the townships. Suggest how this creates wider economic advantages.

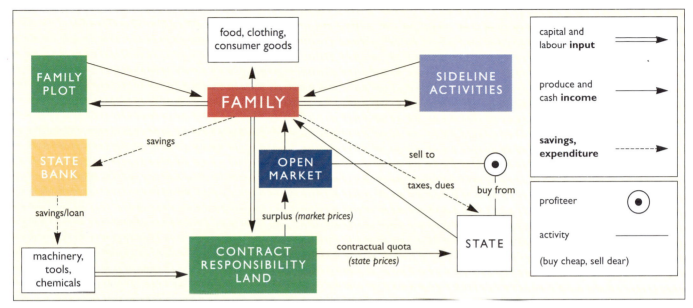

Legend:
- capital and labour **input** →
- produce and cash **income** →
- **savings, expenditure** - - →
- profiteer ⊙
- activity ——
- (buy cheap, sell dear)

Diagram labels: food, clothing, consumer goods; FAMILY PLOT; FAMILY; SIDELINE ACTIVITIES; savings; STATE BANK; OPEN MARKET; sell to; taxes, dues; buy from; savings/loan; surplus (market prices); machinery, tools, chemicals; CONTRACT RESPONSIBILITY LAND; contractual quota (state prices); STATE

family responsibility leased land grain/growing Ⓛ	proportion of family income – % –

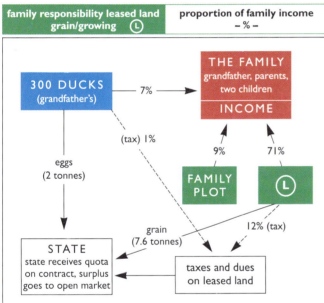

Diagram labels: 300 DUCKS (grandfather's); 7%; THE FAMILY grandfather, parents, two children INCOME; (tax) 1%; eggs (2 tonnes); 9%; 71%; FAMILY PLOT; Ⓛ; grain (7.6 tonnes); 12% (tax); STATE state receives quota on contract, surplus goes to open market; taxes and dues on leased land

Figure 2.22 *(above)* The opportunity for a contracting farming family to save and invest (also a loophole used by entrepreneurs).

Figure 2.23 *(left)* The whole family can contribute and may sell various produce directly on the open market

Nevertheless, a great advantage of the open market over the commune system has been that every member of the family may be profitably involved and contribute directly, as shown in Figure 2.23, or indirectly through employment in township enterprises. There is, however, the danger that as families become profitably involved in outside activities they may minimalise their work on the land, leading to an overall fall in agricultural productivity.

Rural responses to the market economy

A family can lease land on contract, paying dues and tax on sales, and also receive an income from those not employed directly on the land. Savings have allowed more families and collectives to purchase machinery and fertilisers – though not all use them wisely, to the detriment of soils in the long run.

Increases in the price of machinery and chemicals have made farming less attractive for some families. Also, when the Government has contracted to purchase quantities of grain, state prices have been low compared with those on the open market – partly to keep down costs in the cities. This has also allowed some individuals, including officials, to manipulate purchases and sales for their own profit.

Figure 2.24 Older members of the family can contribute by helping to sell surplus produce

Rural-urban contrasts

- Rural communities: adapting to change

- Opportunities vary for rural communities

- The cities: adapting to rapid changes

- Urbanisation: regional characteristics

- Municipalities: Beijing and Tianjin

- Shanghai and its developing hinterland

- The Special Economic Zones

- Social changes: statistical indications

PART 3

Rural communities: adapting to change

Regional conditions and opportunities for peasant farmers vary considerably (page 34), but, overall, introducing the responsibility system dramatically increased rural productivity. Families could now contract, through a township committee, to lease and cultivate land; sell a quota of their produce to the state at agreed prices and the rest on the open market; or arrange to engage in other activities, such as fishing, forestry or brickmaking, or establish light manufacturing. They could make decisions on what to grow beyond their contracted amount, and become involved in marketing. The market system now allows a choice of crops, pooling land by adjusting contracts, and the opportunity to employ labour.

More efficient farming

It pays to invest in improving techniques and in simple machinery like the ubiquitous mini-tractor, now manufactured in a number of regional centres. Where individuals find this difficult, families may come together and contract as a collective unit to cultivate a wider area, using profits to acquire machinery, pumps, pesticides, etc. State banks make loans where appropriate.

Figure 3.1 Consolidation of properties allows co-operative groups to afford machinery, like this tractor ploughing canalside fields south of Chengdu

Figure 3.2 *(far left)* A former commune employee, now an enthusiastic pig-breeder entirely responsible for several dozen animals (**Figure 3.3** *(right)*), enjoys a great increase in income

At county level there are specialists in rural technology who can advise on suitable machinery or new ways of tackling perennial problems, such as crop disease, pests, or erosion. They also advise groups specialising in, say, duck farming, forestry, or tractor maintenance, whose earnings are linked to output or results. One outcome, however, has been an increasing use of chemical fertilisers, which can pose long-term problems for the soils.

China has long had a policy of '**walking on two legs**', using *high technology* where appropriate, but advocating efficient *intermediate technology*, where, for instance, the use of simple machinery and abundant human energy may save fuel. The widespread use of handcarts may suggest rural poverty but, as with animal transport, these are usually equipped with serviceable tyres and efficient axles and bearings. Intensive vegetable cultivation is a feature of rural, and even urban, life with applications of humus, ditch refuse, and animal and human wastes, sometimes as small concentrated briquettes. By contrast, high technology can be introduced where appropriate; for instance providing strains of rice scientifically adapted for rapid growth under regional light conditions – invaluable where a second crop must follow immediately.

Problems under the market system

A large proportion of produce is now sold on the open market, though freedom to choose can cause problems. In some areas grain production has fallen as people have turned to vegetable growing, fruit farming or other activities likely to generate a higher income than grain. The state can still control prices, but giving grain-growers better returns can make grain more expensive for urban consumers and lead to subsidies to reduce the price in urban markets. Also large wholesale markets are being established across the country, with considerable effects on costs. If prices of the produce fall, and if the price of farm equipment and fertilisers is not controlled, rural people may engage in other activities or migrate to nearby towns or further afield.

Rural settlements now contain small firms, factories and workshops, open markets, co-operative stores and small shops with traders offering a wide range of consumer goods. Clothing, in greater variety, can be seen to reflect economic status. Unfortunately, opportunities for unfair profiteering by entrepreneurs, and even by officials, now exist, with instances of contract grain purchased cheaply and then sold locally at higher market rates.

With an increasing rural population, yet fewer needed on the land, there is now migration to towns, where more and more people are engaged in private enterprises. Unfortunately there is also the massive migration of tens of millions from the countryside to seek work in the eastern coastal zone. This again emphasises the need to introduce preferential policies for poorer areas and to reduce the imbalance of economic development.

Availability of social services

Taxes on land and enterprise earnings vary among the provinces, which also pass down subsidies for local purposes. Certain services and welfare amenities are subsidised at a local level, but for many services, including hospital treatment, people pay a contribution. Local paramedics continue to give simple treatment, and theoretically the market economy system now allows private

Figure 3.5 Meat sales on the open market, where the freedom to shop around can generate a queue ... and criticism as here in West Kunming

medical practice; but availability varies with location, and there are indications that with privatisation health care has become less effective.

This also applies to education, which is compulsory up to middle school level, with small contributions for meals, books and tuition. Children attend primary and junior-middle schools and can, in theory, move on for secondary education and compete for places at colleges and higher technical institutes. But in peasant communities, where there are few trained teachers, the children, often involved in farm work during busy seasons, are disadvantaged. Some families remove them from school at primary level. Day-to-day activities and opportunities for rural families vary greatly with location (page 34).

Figure 3.4 Terraced wheat is being harvested among Sichuan's western mountains, with rice seedbeds alongside. China researches, supplies, and exports species adapted to particular light conditions and growing periods

In Focus ....

- 'Poverty is caused by a lack of technology'. Is this a far too sweeping statement?

- Suggest why introducing high technology at village level has disadvantages as well as advantages.

- Why should the introduction of the responsibility system tend to make farming less labour-intensive?

- Consider why fluctuations in China's annual grain production are not entirely due to climatic causes.

- In the 1950s there was 1800 m² of arable land per person. Today there is less than 900 m². Consider the significance of these figures and possible reasons for the decrease.

*O*pportunities vary for rural communities

Different circumstances, different responses

In such a large country, with regional variations in relief, climate, and soil properties, there are obviously great contrasts in rural activities, farming methods, and social activity. Certainly there is no such thing as a 'typical Chinese farming family'. Also, no matter how efficiently people farm, economic opportunities depend on market access; on the nature of that market; and on the available forms of transport and infrastructure. Even in favourable locations, where the change to an open market policy has raised production, increasing mechanisation can mean fewer people are needed to work the land. Local sideline occupations can be profitable, though the size of local markets may limit opportunities.

Apart from general climatic constraints, which may favour pastoral rather than agricultural land use, or wheat rather than rice, there are often dominant local influences of relief, aspect and soil quality. Figure 3.7 shows steep valley sides in western Sichuan where skillful terracing provides a large area of carefully maintained soil capable of supporting a succession of crops. In the main valley below, where cold air accumulates in winter, the riverside terraces only bear a single summer crop, and there are cattle pastures on the gravelly floodplain. The people farm with great efficiency,

Figure 3.7 *(top)* An intricate system of terracing in the western mountains of Sichuan, which provides sufficient stable soil to support sizeable communities. In **Figure 3.8** *(bottom)* a closer view of the terracing reveals variation in seasonal land use. Notice the water outlets from field to field, blocked by stones

but in a remote location such as this can do little to raise their moderate standard of living.

By contrast, further east, in the climatically benign Sichuan Basin generations of farming families have benefited from large-scale irrigation (Figure 5.12, page 62). Water from the Min River was originally diverted to canals in the

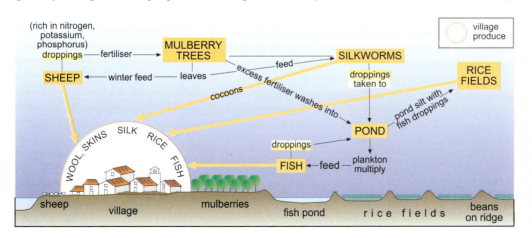

Figure 3.6 *(left)* Villagers evolved a system of sericulture combined with rice, vegetables, fish stocking and sheep grazing, in which each product gains by association with the others

third century BC. These have been progressively extended, and today co-ordinated canal systems help to make this one of China's richest, if over-populated, regions.

There are innumerable differences in day-to-day life among the huge rural population, though common techniques have been inherited and give the landscapes unique Chinese characteristics. Some practices become widespread because of proved efficiency; for example combining sericulture with fish-farming (Figure 3.6) was developed in eastern Guangdong but has been widely used in other silk-producing regions.

Ethnic diversity also creates patterns in land use. The minority peoples in the western mountains, millions in all, are among the poorest. They form cohesive societies with their own traditions, and do not readily migrate; though where potentially cultivable land is developed, there tends to be an influx of Han Chinese. This has happened on a large scale in Nei Mongol where only a small proportion of the pastoral land converted for agriculture is occupied by Mongol farmers.

The influence of the market

However efficient local practices may be, incomes in relatively isolated communities remain low compared with earnings of farmers close to markets, especially those adjoining a large urban area. Figure 3.10 shows the type of intensive agriculture on the outskirts of a city which can benefit families, co-operative communities, and even absentee landholders. Here appropriate techniques and mechanisation can be adopted to an extent impossible for the majority of peasant farmers.

Figure 3.10 Intensive farming on the outskirts of Chengdu. Hardly any land is unproductive, with channels carefully maintained, poles meticulously positioned, and crops rotated with inputs of fertiliser. With a huge local market and low transport costs, conditions and rewards are completely different from those of the mountain farmers (Figure 3.7).

In Guangdong, in the Xi River delta in particular, many farmers have switched from growing grain to producing vegetables and livestock for the urban market. Those with accumulated capital set up small businesses or services. Overseas Chinese, especially from Hong Kong, are involved in such enterprises and employ casual workers. This attracts surplus migratory labour from the interior of the country, where fewer members of a family are needed on the land. Today young women as well as men migrate long distances for work, and many new businesses about Guangzhou and Shenzhen recruit female labour from a wide area for their skills in mass-producing light artifacts for export (Figure 3.9).

Figure 3.9 Women decorating pottery in one of many similar enterprises near Foshan, in the Xi delta, which recruit from a wide area

In Focus ....

● Minority groups, often in marginal areas, face a dilemma in their drive for local autonomy and a degree of independence while wanting economic growth. Consider the difficulty of providing economic opportunities similar to those of other Chinese nationals without infringing beliefs and customs.

● The quality of life in rural China has improved, yet the gap between many parts of the interior and the coastal regions has widened. Consider why coastal development exerts both a 'pull effect' and a 'spread effect', and whether these two effects may coincide.

The cities: adapting to rapid changes

Restructuring the old cities

Figure 1.22 on page 16 shows some of the largest cities, each with at least 1 million people, while tens of millions live in the metropolitan areas. From the outset the PRC's urban population grew rapidly as young families migrated from uncertain rural futures; and with better health facilities the urban death rate was comparatively low. As the focus of roads and railways, provincial capitals were the key centres for industrial development and grew to several times the size of the next largest city. There were soon problems of overcrowding, with pressure on housing, water supply, sewerage systems and the narrow streets. In most of the cities ancient walls and historic sites were removed to provide space for public buildings, offices, widened roads and squares – though today some old streets with small terraced houses may still surround the inner city.

As new arrivals and natural increase led to high unemployment, in-migration was controlled. Also many young people completing secondary education were directed to nearby communes, and others further afield. Today members of rural and urban families are able to migrate, though this also causes considerable problems.

Housing the growing population

Housing blocks with numerous family apartments, very small by Western standards, are now common urban features. State subsidies kept rents low, but a rapidly growing population made financing public housing a burden, and so building began to be restricted. To counter this there is now public investment in housing, with real-estate development agencies, housing co-operatives in which individuals can invest, and factories with housing construction projects partly funded by workers. There are, however, complications, for while state houses and apartments can be sold at low, affordable prices, new houses are considerably more expensive to construct.

In the suburbs high-rise flats cluster about factories, sometimes forming a neighbourhood unit, with schools, shops and public parks. Where spreading suburbs have taken in villages and farmland, factories and flats mingle with areas of intensive cultivation. Rural areas around the city are intensively farmed, and expanses of plastic-covered greenhouses border most northern cities, so that urban spread is a problem. The state-administered Municipalities (page 40) include satellite industrial towns which relieve pressure on the city, preserve its outer boundaries, and help to avoid the shanty developments common to cities in most developing countries.

Providing social services

Urban populations continue to grow, only partly countered by the one-child-only campaign. There is now mobility of labour, with people seeking and switching jobs, and large numbers leaving the countryside for the cities. Despite the proliferation of small enterprises and sideline activities (Figure 6.18, page 84), there is high unemployment.

Groups of streets within the city have formed neighbourhood units, with appointed committees supervising health services and social amenities and keeping watch on local discipline and political affiliations. But

Figure 3.11 Great variation in accommodation in Shanghai. As large cities spread it is more difficult to maintain district administration

Figure 3.12 As cities expand they absorb adjacent villages, though frequently intensive farming continues in open spaces, as here in the outskirts of Kunming

Figure 3.14 Beyond Chang-an Avenue tall offices and flats rise above the older administrative buildings of central Beijing

Figure 3.15 Waiting for a passenger in Urumj in the far west: cities modernise, transport changes!

controlling the lifestyle of young people, many unemployed, and monitoring the activities of entrepreneurs and casual workers, is now beyond their capability and social welfare provisions have had to be reviewed. Employees in state industries have had free medical care and pensions provided by subsidies, but this scale of social welfare is increasingly untenable. Some businesses now arrange joint medical insurance contributions from employers, employees and the state, with funds accumulating for pensions. However, an overall social security system does not exist and different systems operate in different provinces and municipalities. Some aim to build up employment relief funds, despite the numbers involved.

There has always been public concern for the old. In parks early morning visitors perform the slow rhythmic movements of *tai ji quan*, play groups are supervised while parents work, and sites are often reserved for the elderly. But

the population is ageing, which means there is a need for financial planning to meet a retirement boom, especially as the one-child policy destroys the extended family.

There is growing traffic in the city streets. Although there are still relatively few private cars, there is plentiful public transport, numerous taxis and trucks serving factories, department stores and markets. Many cities are constructing or extending ring roads and expressways (Figure 3.24). Nevertheless, cycles by the million remain the customary form of transport, parked in orderly rows by stores and offices.

Market influences and new enterprises in secondary and tertiary industries are thus rapidly changing the cities, although each retains special characteristics related to its location and functions. By contrast, the new, planned, urban-industrial cities in the Special Economic Zones bear little resemblance to the older towns and cities (page 44).

Figure 3.13 A corner of Green Park in Kunming set aside for older citizens, here playing cards

In Focus ....

● Compared with the days of controlled population movement there is now greater freedom and for most the quality of life has undoubtedly improved. Yet there seems to be a growing sense of insecurity among the urban populations. Suggest reasons for this.

*U*rbanisation: regional characteristics

Figure 3.17 Kunming expands along the lowland bordering Lake Dian, with characteristic greenery among a network of well-proportioned flats

Unique urban features

China's urban characteristics vary considerably according to location, site, historical background, regional assets and accessibility from the main zones of economic development. In many Chinese cities ancient sites still affect the urban structure, perhaps constraining modern activities but often acting as valuable tourist attractions. Today, Government decisions on urban development exert major influences: certain cities are targeted for improvements to attract foreign investors with particular interest in commercial activities, establishing industrial enterprises, or developing sources of energy.

Despite the intrusive factories, concrete flats and peripheral industrial zones which make for characterless uniformity, most of the major cities have unique features, and the following examples show that regional cities may undergo economic development and yet retain their distinctive character.

Figure 3.16 Xian, with its ancient walls and moat and, typical of northern cities, open spaces with lines of plastic-covered greenhouses. Manufacturing industries have spread beyond the walls and there are now industrial parks with new hi-tech enterprises

The variety of cities

There are great differences between the ambience of a subtropical city such as Kunming, bordering the scenic Lake Dian, high on the list of popular tourist attractions, and Shenyang, heavy-industrial freight centre of the North East, a Mecca for steam railway enthusiasts. This difference can be attributed to latitude, local topography, and relative access to minerals: but political and economic factors also influence when and how each city acquires its particular functions (pages 56 and 64). Similarly, an historical perspective will show why Wuhan and Nanjing, two dominant city ports on the Chang jiang with comparable populations and many industrial functions in common, have such different urban characteristics. Wuhan justifies the description of an industrial conglomerate (page 67), and Nanjing, former capital of the southern Song, that of a green and pleasant city, flaunting its ancient walls, and still a major cultural centre (page 68).

A comparison of three provincial capitals, each targeted for investment to stimulate economic spread in the interior, emphasises that Chinese cities should be studied in a regional context.

Xian, in the fertile loess lands, inherited the administrative role of ancient Chang'an, and retains the rectangular outer walls which enclosed the grid of streets and avenues and its socially differentiated districts. Under the Sui and Tang dynasties it was the imperial centre of commerce and culture, before its decline to regional status.

By the nineteenth century Xian had become a somewhat isolated provincial city; in fact the railway to Zhengzhou, on the lower Huang He, was not completed until 1930. But as the PRC began to industrialise the city and irrigate the countryside around it, Xian regained regional dominance. Its industries at first reflected rural productivity and local demands, producing textiles, electrical machinery, fertilisers and consumer goods. Now it is a city of 3 million people with universities, research institutes and hi-tech industries and acts as a satellite control base. Yet it also prospers from its history: its walls and gates and proximity to imperial splendours make Xian one of China's prime tourism centres.

Taiyuan, in the Fen valley, capital of Shanxi province, also has a remarkable historical background (page 59). It is acquiring a growing number of hi-tech industries, also monitors satellites and acts as a tourism centre; yet it is a completely different city from Xian. With manufacturing functions based on coal, iron ore, and cotton, it rather resembles more of a Lancastrian city emerging from the industrial infrastructure of its Victorian heyday. Modern blocks of flats and concrete commercial buildings rise among the small workers' houses and courtyards and chimneys of the older factories (Figure 3.19).

Chengdu, the capital of Sichuan, renowned over its 2500 year history for arts, crafts, and the quality of its silks, now has foreign investment in electronic, metallurgical and machine-building industries. Multi-storey department stores, fashion shops, and ring road infrastructure demonstrate its present affluence. Yet Chengdu is also a green city with flowering shrubs, overhanging wooden housing in old streets which accommodate small merchants and artisans, and ancient spice markets. Nationally influential, it administers China's most populous province (page 62) yet retains historical and regional characteristics.

Quite apart from these three cities are the new urban-industrial clusters which most dramatically reflect China's recent economic surge – those in the Special Economic Zones (SEZs) (page 44). They, too, differ from each other in many respects. Shenzhen, for instance, has been

Figure 3.19 (above) Textile factories in Taiyuan, which developed as an industrial city close to Shanxi's reserves of coal and iron ore

Figure 3.20 (left) Terraced workers' houses surround old factories and newer flats in central Taiyuan

Figure 3.21 (right) Quiet streets, with old houses and small workshops, beyond the opulent centre of Chengdu

developed in recent years to function solely as a ready-made modern metropolis, attracting international business enterprises and financial institutions; Xiamen on the other hand was a thriving port in imperial times but has now, as an SEZ, become a high-rise commercial city with modern industrial estates.

Figure 3.18 In this flowery central business district of Chengdu, the capital of Sichuan, there are now towering shopping complexes

In Focus ....

● How does this brief introduction (pages 36-9) emphasise that an urban settlement should be regarded as a 'human environment', subject to evolution and change, particularly in the case of Chinese cities?

● In the 1980s China aimed to promote the growth of small cities, develop medium size ones, and control the growth of major cities. In fact the latter have expanded, and during that decade the number of 'million' cities doubled. Consider why this was due partly to the policy of attracting foreign investment, and partly to a surplus workforce in rural areas.

Municipalities: Beijing and Tianjin

Figure 3.23 High-rise flats and many of the newer industries spread out towards the Summer Palace in north west Beijing

Beijing

The state of China directly administers three great Municipalities – Beijing, Tianjin, and Shanghai – this includes control of areas far beyond the city suburbs. The Municipality of Beijing, with a population of about 12 million, extends over lowlands inland of Bohai and into the mountains beyond the Great Wall. There is administrative control over: a) the city itself, with some 7 million people; b) the rural areas supplying fresh produce to the urban core; c) the satellite towns with their own industrial development; d) large reservoirs; e) historical sites, in and beyond the city, bringing a large income from tourism; and f) road, rail, and air communications.

The oldest parts of Beijing were built during the Ming Dynasty. The walls have mostly gone, but among the imperial remains stands the Forbidden City, surrounded by a moat. Its southern gate (Tiananmen) faces the square of the same name, created early in the century and scene of politically significant rallies and demonstrations.

Beijing is a modern political and cultural capital with a range of heavy and light engineering, hi-tech and consumer-orientated industries, and increasingly sophisticated *tertiary industries*, served by a road infrastructure superimposed on the traditional grid pattern. Expressways with overpasses and subways form a succession of ring roads around the centre, crossed by trunk roads which extend to the outer suburbs and run north eastwards to the airport. Beyond the city expressways have cut the journey times to Tianjin and Shijiazhuang (page 58). An underground railway also encircles the city centre, with an extension to the western suburbs.

There is a central concentration of administrative and commercial buildings and hotels, and in the suburbs high-rise blocks overlook the old lanes (*hutongs*) with their courtyard houses. The outer sectors have acquired specific functions: in the north west, for instance, towards the Summer Palace, there are colleges, universities, and research institutes, with numerous hi-tech industries in the western outskirts. 20 km to the west are the steelworks of the Capital Iron and Steel Corporation (Shougang) which supply the Beijing Engine Works and associated automobile and agricultural machinery factories. The Corporation controls steel industries elsewhere in China, distributing foreign ores and imported steel plant. It has also acquired ore fields overseas.

Beijing is thus an administrative–industrial city, with increasing consumerism among people with different income levels. Like other major cities it acts as a magnet, drawing a floating population, which unfortunately results in unemployment problems. Beijing strives to combat air pollution and water shortage: its sulphurous coal-burning factories and house-fires have been notorious polluters, and the introduction of natural gas piped 900 km from Shaanxi province (page 60) will be a boon to the whole city.

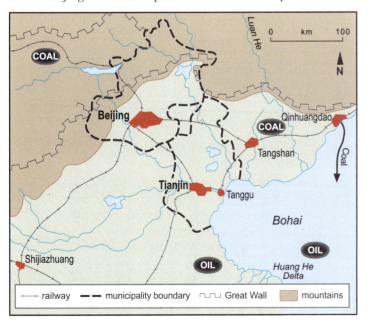

Figure 3.22 The broad Municipalities of Beijing and Tianjin

Figure 3.24 *(below)* Beijing's ring roads are now multi-lane highways around the city centre. Trees show the deliberate 'greening' of many of the large cities

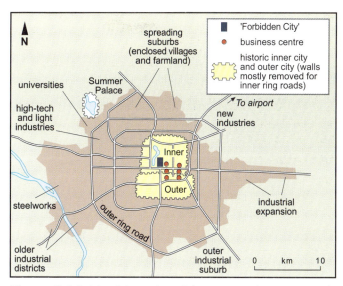

Figure 3.26 *(above)* An outline of the major road system around the historic centre of Beijing, from which expressways extend eastward and southward

In the outer metropolis various rural enterprises are involved in intensive farming. Some villages have co-operative systems for cultivation and marketing, and as living standards rise and demands increase they are setting-up self-funded industrial enterprises. Several million tourists visit the metropolis each year, and the outer historic sites are still major attractions: notably the Great Wall restored under the Ming: the tombs of the Ming emperors; Chengde, the Qing imperial resort; and the Summer Palace.

Tianjin

Tianjin, like Beijing, is administered as a wider municipality of some 10 million people, with intensively cultivated farmlands about the city port. It developed, as a textile manufacturing city, near the confluence of five tributaries to the Hai River, and because of local silting has progressively constructed and enlarged new ports 50 km downstream. The whole area is now a coastal development zone, with the new harbour, Tanggu-Xingang, China's main container port.

Drawing energy from a region rich in coal, gas, and oil,

Tianjin's industries range from heavy machinery and vehicle manufacturing to hundreds of firms making hi-tech products such as precision electronics apparatus and quality consumer goods. These are backed by scientific research and increasing foreign investment.

Tianjin's manufacturing enterprises, wholesale markets, shopping districts and research institutes are served by a modern road network and subway. Much of the reconstruction followed earthquake damage in 1976, when nearby Tangshan was destroyed. Unfortunately the city has a long-standing water shortage, only partly solved by massive tunnelling to bring supplies from the Luan He, far to the north. As with Beijing, demand has increased, and there are now plans to obtain water for both cities from a distant reservoir in Hubei province, fed by the Han River.

Figure 3.25 North of Beijing the Ming Azure Clouds Temple and Fragrant Hills gardens attract tourists and local people alike

In Focus ....

● In Municipalities the relationships between the large cities and the rural areas are particularly significant. Consider reasons for the sequence of development projects at the village level put forward by Beijing's Institute of Environmental Protection: agricultural diversification to include poultry farming, dairying and vegetable production; investment in greenhouses, sprinkler irrigation, feed processing, and plant to pipe biogas to houses and workplaces; trees to surround villages and fields; a depot for trucks and machine maintenance.

● Explain why the increasing population and rapid economic growth of the city calls for investment in enterprises both within and beyond the Municipality.

Shanghai, and its developing hinterland

The municipality of Shanghai, with 14 million people, lies at the outlet of the 'economic corridor' of the Chang jiang, and includes Chongming Island. Its core is the densely populated city port about the Huangpu, an international commercial and financial centre, with a stock exchange, colleges, technical institutes, and thousands of factories with satellite industrial settlements about the city proper. Shanghai manufactures many of China's foremost industrial products (steel, machine tools, cotton textiles and artificial fibres), and turns out consumer goods for the huge domestic market. It also has a growing number of specialist hi-tech enterprises.

The city centre is 28 km from the mouth of the Huangpu. Here the Wusong River (Suzhou Creek) provides a waterway westward through the city. The former British dominated International Settlement was here, with a French Concession nearby. Foreign commercial buildings lined the Bund, overlooking the Huangpu, for European interests made this the country's chief commercial and banking centre and the gateway to a huge internal market. Docks were built

downstream, and industries, such as cotton textiles, were established around the port area, backed by a dense jumble of small buildings – unplanned slums, inadequately supplied with drinking water and sewerage.

The Municipality is divided into 12 districts, including the rural areas to the west. Parts of the inner district have regained something of Shanghai's former cosmopolitan atmosphere, with international firms in office blocks, departments stores, hotels and entertainment facilities and increasing employment in tertiary industries. About 8 million people live in the overcrowded inner city, where slow-moving traffic adds fumes to the smoke pollution. Apartment blocks tower over renovated housing in the maze

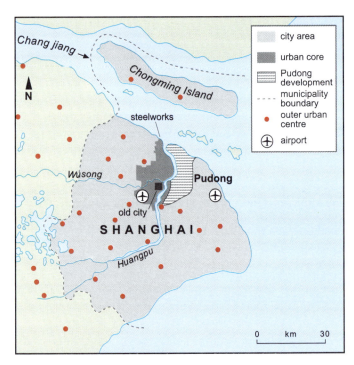

Figure 3.28 The municipality of Shanghai with spreading urban-industrial areas circling the city core and the planned development of Pudong across the Huangpu

Figure 3.27 Shanghai's Bund, the solid financial and commercial buildings established in the days of foreign concessions, now backed by modern office blocks

of narrow streets, and in-migration increases the crowding in what, despite the provision of schools, recreation spaces, and the preservation of parks, remains a congested area. Waste disposal is a considerable problem, though there is a new sewage system with outlet to the ocean, and the heavily polluted Suzhou Creek is now being treated.

In the outer western suburbs new residential areas mingle with clusters of factories and research centres. Each neighbourhood has markets, stores, medical centres and schools. Trucks bring fresh produce from outer farmholdings, where entrepreneurs produce successive vegetable crops by intensive methods. Buses and innumerable cycles, adding to the traffic, carry people to central businesses and stores which now offer a wide choice of goods. An underground railway system and a 40 km ring road are helping to ease traffic problems. The industrial satellite towns have absorbed several million people and provide employment in factories producing modern consumer goods, such as textiles, refrigerators and TVs, and have set up hi-tech industries, including the construction of rockets used to launch space satellites.

The Pudong development

Along the Huangpu, with its factories, wharfs and container terminals, ships supply materials to the Baoshan integrated steelworks near the mouth, and to shipyards and thermal power stations. There are oil and petrochemical industries on the east bank and here the Pudong New Area is being developed with massive foreign and domestic investment, as a financial centre and industrial zone with a customs-free port. Each of its sub districts, housing hundreds of thousands, has specific activities: one district for financial/administration; another for scientific research; while the container port is backed by hi-tech and processing industries; and there is also a non-polluting industrial zone.

Figure 3.30 Nanjing Road in Shanghai, packed with pedestrians, public transport and light industrial vehicles

Accommodation is mostly in tower blocks with nearby service facilities. A second international airport is under construction on Pudong and the whole area is connected to the main part of the city by road bridges and tunnels.

The development of Shanghai and the delta area is related to the wider policy of extending economic advantages and foreign investment into the hinterland. This development is achieved by stimulating growth in cities along the 'Chang jiang corridor', with the prospect of help from the Three Gorges Project (page 54).

In Focus ....

● What are the advantages of administering Beijing, Tianjin, and Shanghai as municipal areas rather than just urban concentrations?

● Suggest why, compared with provinces, these three municipalities have such a high proportion of their workforce in secondary and tertiary industries .

Figure 3.29 A passenger vessel joins numerous merchant ships along the Huangpu, where industrial development extends along both banks

The Special Economic Zones

Figure 3.32 In Shenzhen, Chinese and foreign firms manufacture a range of electronic products, both for export and the home market

The eastern, coastal part of China has nearly two-thirds of the country's industrial production, contributes 80 per cent of its export earnings, and receives 90 per cent of its foreign capital input. With the existing advantages and international accessibility, the aim is to stimulate further economic growth and eventually achieve a spread effect, using created wealth to assist the interior. Certain eastern localities – ports and industrial-agricultural areas – are targeted to achieve rapid economic growth.

The Special Economic Zones

Shenzhen, Zhuhai, Shantou, Xiamen and Hainan have been established as Special Economic Zones (SEZs) to attract foreign business ventures and investment, through tax incentives, reduced tariffs, flexible labour and the advantages of modern infrastructure. There is particular encouragement for industries which will bring in foreign currency. The expertise in technology and management associated with foreign firms and joint Chinese-foreign enterprises can also be transferred to benefit home manufacturing generally.

Shenzhen SEZ adjoins Hong Kong's New Territories and is linked by road and rail to Guangzhou. Since 1980 a high-rise industrial–financial zone has been developed around this small town, with thousands of co-operative businesses, joint ventures, foreign-owned enterprises, a stock exchange and a population of over 3 million. Many of its industries are hi-tech, involving electronics, while others range from textiles designed to meet foreign demands to vehicle assembly for home markets. Wages and housing conditions above the national average attract skilled workers from all over China. However, wages here and in Guangdong generally are lower than in the 'four tigers' (Taiwan, South Korea, Hong Kong and Singapore), which encourages overseas entrepreneurs, especially Hong Kong business people, to set up firms. Businesses in other parts of the country gain international connections through branches in Shenzhen. Apart from the land routes to central Hong Kong,

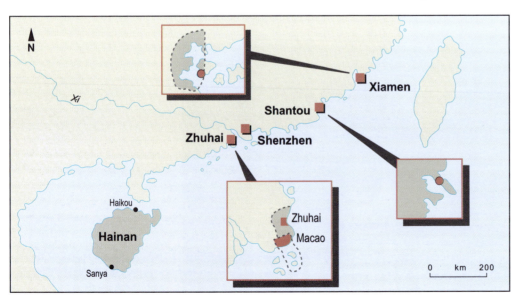

Figure 3.31 The Special Economic Zones: Shenzhen, Zhuhai, and Shantou in Guangdong province; Xiamen in Fujian; and Hainan island province. These are located in the south east, with its many overseas connections; together with Guangzhou and Hong Kong, they make use of foreign capital and technological inputs

Figure 3.33 Shenzhen Zone and City located, with exports in mind, as an economic-industrial link between Guangzhou and Hong Kong. New resorts are now attracting tourists

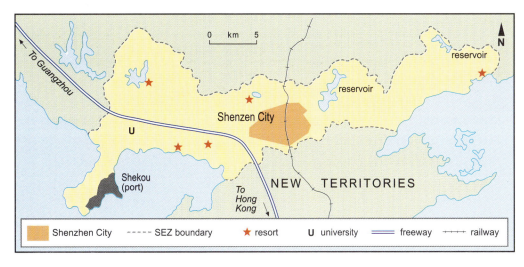

there is an airport at Huangtian and rapid sea links with Hong Kong, Macao, and Zhuhai SEZ through Shenzhen's passenger and cargo port, Shekhou.

Zhuhai SEZ has established a hi-tech industrial zone on a reclaimed sandy wasteland bordering Macao. It is now constructing an airport, extending its deep-water harbour, and considering a 50 km bridge link with Hong Kong. Like Shenzhen it has tourist facilities, and has developed a large holiday complex.

Shantou, on Guangdong's northern, rugged coast, once just a small port about a river estuary, is now an SEZ with industrial parks, container terminal, and airport. Here many Overseas Chinese have returned and are investing in export industries, especially in clothing aimed at specific overseas markets.

Xiamen SEZ has developed around an island linked by road and rail bridge to the Fujian coast. A port since Ming times, it later served European interests, acquiring an array of consulates, though there was little foreign investment until the 1980s. It is now a bustling city, with a new port well-placed for trade with Hong Kong, South East Asia, and Taiwan. The zone specialises in scientific research, with thousands of foreign-backed enterprises, whose products include TVs, electronic and photographic equipment. Many of the investors are Taiwanese, both overseas and resident.

Hainan Island, the largest SEZ, became a province in 1988. It has attracted foreign investment in building its development area infrastructure, as well as in manufacturing. While most foreign enterprises are located about Haikou, the capital, with its port and airport, there is huge international investment in an export-oriented development area with a deep-water harbour, on the Yangpu peninsula. This will concentrate on hi-tech industries. A new airport at Sanya, in the far south, is allowing tourism to develop in a tropical environment.

In 1984 China decided to allow 14 open coastal cities to establish economic development areas to attract foreign interest, especially in technological industries. Most of them now have customs-free zones. Following their rapid economic growth, in 1992 other cities were nominated for accelerated development – those along the Chang jiang corridor, provincial capitals, and certain 'border' cities. Although the country as a whole is now deemed to be open to a market economy, certain privileged development areas are targeted by the state (as with the Chang jiang corridor, page 66), or earmarked by provinces, as eligible for measures to stimulate rapid economic growth.

In Focus ....

● Why do Overseas Chinese with experience of the rise of newly industrialising countries (NICs) like the 'four tigers' look to invest in Chinese enterprises, and how can they contribute to China's economic development drive?

Figure 3.34 Part of the central business district of Shenzhen highlights the great differences in lifestyles within China (cf Figure 2.18, page 28)

Figure 3.35 Statistical indicators

SOCIAL PROGRESS INDICATORS						
Indicators	Cities		Indicators	Villages		
	1980	1990		1980	1990
Protein/capita (g/day)	60	67	Protein/capita (g/day)	47	60
Average lifespan (yr)	67	70	Average lifespan (yr)	68	70
Housing area/capita (m²)	4	7	With good roads (%)	50	74
Ratio of tertiary industry (%)	21	30	Households with electricity (%)	50	86
Middle school attendance (%)	70	92	Steel/wood frame houses (%)	43	62
Park (green space)/capita (m²)	3	7	TV sets/100 households	1	44
Income/capita gain 1980-90 (%)	–	105	'Safe' water available (%)	50	70

The gap between China's cities and villages is immense. The State Statistical Bureau has examined various indicators of social progress between 1980 and 1990, a selection of which are shown in Figure 3.35.

Statistics must be treated with caution because they can give misleading impressions of absolute progress, or otherwise. As indicated in Figure 3.4 (page 33), cultivation by peasants or collective groups can be meticulous and efficient. **Unit productivity** of grain has risen from 1.2 tonnes per hectare in the 1950s to 4.0 tonnes in the 1990s. Yet figures of **labour productivity** (grain volume ÷ agricultural labour force) have changed little over that period: for although in 40 years grain production rose from 160 million tonnes to 440 million tonnes (in 1992), the agricultural labour force increased from less than 200 million to over 400 million.

Figure 3.36 shows the national population pyramid, including figures from the 1990 census. Notice the events and policy changes which have affected its shape.

At A the bulge indicates the baby boom, when political stability returned to a newly established nation. B points to the disaster period of the 'Great Leap Forward', the break with the USSR, and climatic variations, when millions died of starvation. C shows a period of recovery, erratic during the Cultural Revolution, but sufficient to stimulate population control. D illustrates the decline due to the one-child policy. E reflects a relaxation of the policy for farming families, and possibly of less strict observation by sections of the population.

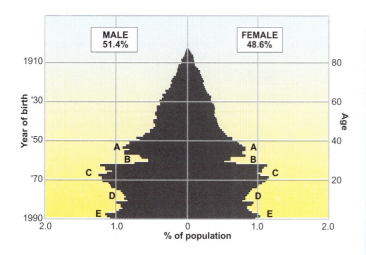

Figure 3.36 The fluctuations in population since the establishment of The People's Republic reflect the consequences of political policies and climatic abnormalities

In Focus ....

- Why are many factors chosen to indicate changes in urban areas irrelevant to conditions in villages, and why would a figure of 'annual earnings per capita' for 'average' rural families be unrealistic and tell relatively little of rural productivity and living standards?

- The overall population of consumers is increasing by some 16 million a year, urban populations are growing rapidly, and rising living standards make for greater demands. Consider the impact of the demands that China is making on world food sources, already stretched by a growing global population.

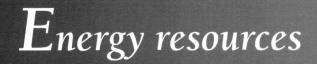

Energy resources

- **Energy: demands and availability**

- **Energy from fossil fuels**

- **Hydro-electric power and nuclear potential**

- **The Three Gorges Project**

PART 4

Energy: demands and availability

Figure 4.2 The all-purpose mini-tractor. As mechanisation increases so do demands for energy, machine production, maintenance, and fuel

Meeting growing demands

Insufficient energy supplies is one of the greatest threats to China's economic growth. There are very large reserves of coal, productive and potentially productive oilfields, though some have passed their peak production capacity, and considerable untapped hydro-electric potential. Demands for energy continue to increase, from consumers in expanding towns and cities, from large manufacturing industries, and from the growing number of small factories and from processing plants in towns. Rural mechanisation and the widespread use of electric pumps for drainage, irrigation and water supply add to demands.

Power stations feed local and regional grids, but the country is too large for a fully integrated electric grid system. Nevertheless, as the interior is opened up and industrialisation spreads, there needs to be a wider distribution of energy generation. For instance, even with hydro-electric energy from the Gezhouba Dam, the 'economic growth corridor' about the Chang jiang has inadequate supplies (page 66) – though the Three Gorges Project aims to remedy this.

Unfortunately, the production, distribution and use of energy have been inefficient, particularly in the case of coal. Underfunding, poor technology, lack of expertise in management and employees, and the size of the country with its large rural population have all contributed to making energy shortage one of the principal constraints for the Chinese economy. As a result, China now welcomes foreign participation in funding major power projects (pages 50-2), providing experts in modern management and technology, and also locating and developing new resources. In fact making coal output more efficient and finding adequate oil reserves are essential for the scale of urban-industrialisation needed to make China a middle-income country free from the burden of massive energy imports.

Harnessing local sources

The rural population benefits from the policy of 'walking on two legs'. This uses both high technology for generation and distribution on a large scale and efficient intermediate

Figure 4.1 A 'wirescape' close to Chongqing emphasises the increasing demands for energy in the flats with their TV aerials, and the small factories, which are now mushrooming in rural townships

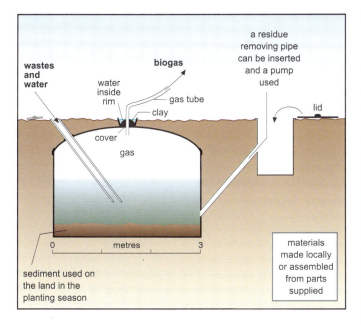

sediment used on
the land in the
planting season

Figure 4.3 *(left)* The generation of methane from organic waste is widespread, though less effective during the winter in northern provinces. Digesters can be constructed to serve a family or, on a larger scale, a community

Figure 4.4 *(below)* Lime kilns, of traditional construction, and new factories, built in response to a surge in population, add to energy demands in a relatively remote part of eastern Yunnan

technology to produce energy from local sources. Numerous small hydro-electric generators on local rivers and streams supply rural communities, notably in the moist, rugged country in the south east and south west. Alternative sources of energy, such as wind power (Figure 5.37, page 73) and biogas are also widely harnessed.

The generation of **biogas** in a simple digester provides energy for tens of millions of rural families, and by reducing the use of charcoal helps to conserve woodland. Human and animal wastes and crop residues are converted into methane in a concrete cylinder fitted into a pit, capped by a brick dome and sealed by clay (Figure 4.3). Wastes pass through a pipe into the fermenting mass, and a flexible tube conducts methane to the house, where a valve regulates supplies. The upper residue, rich in plant nutrients, can be siphoned off and sprayed on crops; while the whole is removed at intervals, mixed with ammonia to avoid parasitic infection and added to soils prior to planting. Methane production has indirectly improved sanitation and helped to prevent disease in rural areas. Biogas is also used in rural machinery.

In southern China and in sunny inland regions **solar panels** are being introduced and **solar reflectors** are used by rural communities to concentrate energy for boiling water and cooking. Simple constructions from steel, metal wire, mirrors, concrete, and asphalt, the reflectors need only occasional angular adjustment.

Any locally generated form of energy is valuable in such a large country, where coal or charcoal may have to be carried, natural gas piped or power lines extended over great distances. There are other natural sources, though they are likely to supply relatively small amounts of energy on the national scale. In various parts of the south eastern hill country there are hot springs and *geothermal energy* is

already harnessed at several power stations inland of Shantou. There are thousands of possible sites in south west China alone, but development depends on accessibility, local demands and the provision of a distribution system. The same applies to *tidal power*; for while there are only minor developments on the Zhejiang coast, a large tidal power station is being constructed on the Shandong peninsula, where the economic potential is high.

In Focus ....

- Deciding on an appropriate source of energy and investment in generating plant means considering factors such as the need to create rapid economic growth in an area, the potential of an underdeveloped region, and the increasing number of factories being set up in townships and villages. Why are some areas best served by huge projects, while others prefer investment in many small energy sources?

- How does the fact that much energy is lost by distribution through a grid system highlight the value of 'walking on two legs'?

Energy from fossil fuels

Figure 4.6 A drab coal mining settlement, typical of many about the Fen valley

Coal mining and distribution

Coal supplies about 75 per cent of China's energy from immense reserves, mostly north of the Chang jiang. It is particularly abundant in Shanxi, Nei Mongol and Shaanxi, where there is now foreign investment and adoption of new methods, as in the Sino-American open-cast mining in Shanxi's shallow north-south fields.

Coal has to be transported long distances. For example, Datong, in northern Shanxi, sends coal to Qinhuangdao on the Bohai Gulf, the country's main coal exporter, and supplies steelworks in Beijing, Taiyuan, and Baotou in Nei Mongol. Unfortunately distribution has been hampered by bottle-necks in the railway system, and there is now heavy investment in new routes and in upgrading older ones (page 81). The Datong-Qinhuangdao line has been electrified and double-tracked, as have those to the coal port of Huanghua

further south on Bohai Gulf, and to Qingdao from the coalfields west of the Shandong peninsula.

In the north-eastern provinces immensely thick seams supply power stations and steelworks in the industrial areas, and coal is distributed southwards by rail and coastal shipping. Oilshales overlie coal in a number of fields, and are distilled for oil and oil products, notably at Fushun (Figure 5.2, page 57)

Fortunately there are also large sources of coal far inland. In the far west Xinjiang's abundant reserves are hardly tapped, though they supply industrial developments around Urumji. In the Sichuan Basin coal lies beneath the red sandstones and outcrops on its western margins. With abundant natural gas and its hydro-electric stations, this populous province has a high energy potential.

In central and southern China there is coal in every province, sufficient in Guizhou to export. Some fields are regionally significant, like that at Puqi, which sends coal north by rail to the heavy-industrial city of Wuhan (page 67). However, reserves in southern China are relatively meagre. Small mines may be locally valuable, but mining methods are often crude.

Coal combustion causes serious air pollution, particularly in northern industrial cities where most homes use this fuel.

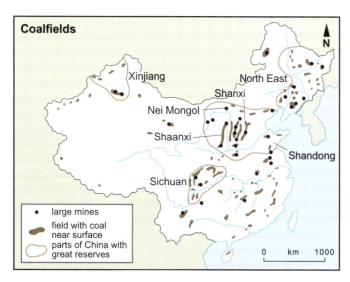

Figure 4.5 The concentration of coal reserves in the North East means a wide and expensive distribution by rail

Figure 4.7 *(right)* Increasing coal output involves co-ordinating transport serving small mines like this, which work rich reserves near Datong, as well as investing in large-scale operations using modern equipment

Sulphur dioxide emissions are high, and stations throughout China monitor acid rain. For this reason alone the decision to pipe natural gas from northern Shaanxi to Xian and Beijing will be environmentally beneficial.

Petroleum and natural gas

Petroleum provides about 20 per cent of the country's energy. With its chemical products, it was until recently a leading export. But with declining production in major fields, falling oil prices, and increasing home consumption, exports decreased, and in 1992 China became a net importing country. Nevertheless there are many productive fields, large reserves in the far west, and an increasing use of foreign capital to locate and exploit new sources of oil and gas. Offshore exploration and development relies heavily on foreign participation. There is already production in Bohai, off the Pearl River estuary, and in the Beibu Wan (Gulf of Tongking), where large natural gas fields will supply both Hainan and Hong Kong. There is also agreement for joint Sino-American exploration and development of sources around the Nansha (Spratly) Islands in the South China Sea, though this is an area of international tension, with territorial claims by other Asian countries.

Figure 4.8 shows the main producing oilfields. Dajing, beneath the north eastern plains, is the most productive, though output has peaked. It pipes oil far to the south and supplies petrochemical works in the industrial cities. Other productive fields fringe the Bohai Gulf. Those at Shengli, near the mouth of the Huang He, have an output second

Figure 4.9 Natural gas plant in a valley in the western mountains exploits one of Sichuan's many productive fields

only to Dajing, while Zhongyuan produces both natural gas and oil, together with the Dagang and Huabei oilfields south of Beijing they pipe oil for export through Qingdao. In fact there is pipeline linkage from Dajing in the far north to the lower Chang jiang, where oil can be transhipped to Wuhan and Shanghai.

Inland, central Sichuan exploits gas and oil reserves located some 200 km north of Chongqing; but it is in the far west that prospecting involving foreign companies continues to reveal really great potential. The Junggar Basin now pipes oil to refineries west of Urumqi, while immense reserves of oil and gas are being found in the Tarim Basin, and refineries have been established on its northern rim. From the Qaidam Basin petroleum goes to refineries at Yumen, which serve nearby oilfields and are linked by pipeline to the oil and chemical complex at Lanzhou.

By contrast, some large coastal refineries use imported oil. Those at Maoming, in the far south east, originally treated local oilshales, but now receive foreign oil piped from Zhanjiang port and export petroleum products.

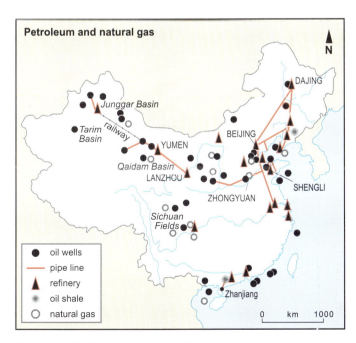

Figure 4.8 The main prospects for large-scale production are in the far west and the offshore fields developed by foreign firms under contract

In Focus ....

- Why does China, in particular, have problems in distributing fossil fuels?

- Large-scale hydro-electric projects are likely to benefit less developed parts of Guangxi and Guizhou provinces (page 70). Why may this also lead to the development of Guizhou's considerable coal reserves?

*H*ydro-electric power and nuclear potential

Investment in hydro-electricity

China has an enormous hydro-electric potential, especially in the south. Many of the feasible sites are far from urban-industrial demands, although harnessing energy in a remote region can encourage development and may fulfil other purposes such as flood control or irrigation. In this way dams in gorges on the upper Huang He not only supply water and energy to industrial Xining and Lanzhou but help to maintain extensive irrigated farmlands. The dam in the Luijia gorge above Lanzhou both reduces summer flooding downstream and later releases water to improve navigation.

Further east, where the Huang He, joined by the Wei, flows through a series of gorges, the multi-purpose Sanmen Dam helps to control flooding and irrigation along the North China plain. Unfortunately the summer silt load has reduced the reservoir's capacity, so that much water is now released through sluices and gorge-side tunnels, and the energy generated, though still large, is below that projected.

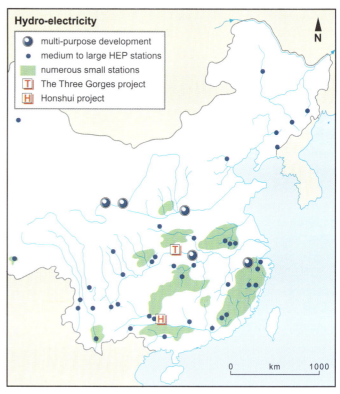

Figure 4.11 Apart from active HEP stations and the huge multi-purpose projects, several regions physically favour the use of small generators

The Chang jiang and its tributaries in Sichuan are also dammed in gorges in the western mountains. The upper river generates energy for the new steel city of Panzhihua and its mineral-rich valley (page 63), while stations on the southward-flowing tributaries supply the densely populated Sichuan Basin. As the Chang jiang emerges from the limestone gorges on the borders of Sichuan and Hubei, energy is generated at the Gezhouba Dam, which also helps to control flooding downriver, where the wide overflow basins have become ineffective.

Figure 4.12 *(below)* Energy from the Dadu Dam stimulates industrial development downriver, backed by typical intensive farming

Figure 4.10 Hydro-electric power is generated at this dam on the Dadu River in western Sichuan

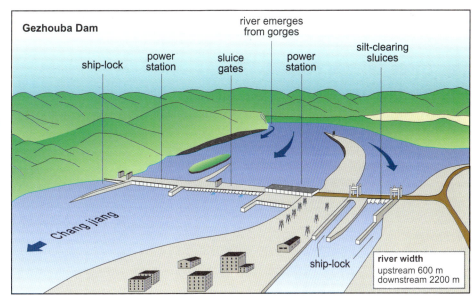

Figure 4.13 Where the Chang jiang emerges from the Three Gorges, the Gezhouba Dam divides the flow into three channels, with two shiplocks and two power stations. It checks only a small proportion of the summer flow, though eventually the Sanxia Dam should alleviate widespread flooding downstream

Over the next decade, with the help of large-scale foreign investment and technology, China aims to develop an immense hydro-electric project which will be vital for economic growth along the river 'corridor'. A 175 m deep reservoir is planned behind the Sanxia Dam (Figure 4.14), extending through the Three Gorges for 660 km, with ship-elevators allowing 11 500 tonne vessels to reach Chongqing during the summer. This involves displacing more than 1 million people, many of whom live in small townships and will require re-housing and re-employment. On completion, the dam should control about half the annual volume of flow of the Chang jiang and reduce flood danger for some 50 million people downriver. The pros and cons of this controversial project are considered on page 54.

Further east, in rugged country south of the Chang jiang delta, the Xinan Dam supplies energy to a grid serving Hangzhou, Nanjing, Shanghai and its immediate hinterland (page 69). These south-eastern hills receive heavy summer rain and have great potential energy. In several locations a high reservoir on a single river supplies a chain of medium-size power stations, while hundreds of tiny generators on local streams provide electricity for rural communities. In eastern Guangdong a number of large hydro-electric stations feed the grid serving Guangzhou and the Xi delta.

In the south west as well, many rural settlements are supplied by small generators. Now large power projects aim to develop neglected hill country in Guangxi, Guizhou and Yunnan. Three out of a proposed chain of ten hydro-electric stations on the Hongshui are already helping to open up country around Luizhou in central Guangxi, which is rich in non-ferrous metals. Further west, in southern Yunnan, five hydro-electric stations are being constructed on the Lancang jiang in a region targeted for economic development. The first two, Manwan and Dachaoshan, are already in operation (page 65).

In north east China dams on the Yalu and Liao Rivers, and further north on the Songhua and its tributaries, create reservoirs deep enough to overcome freezing in the bitter winters. Hydro-electricity helps to boosts energy inputs from thermal stations to the big industrial regions. Deep reservoirs and generators on two rivers to the north east of Beijing supply the city and its surroundings with water and feed electricity to the grid.

Nuclear energy

China's first nuclear power station has been operating at Qinshan, in Zhejiang province, since 1991. Foreign investment and plant were obtained to construct the second station at Daya Bay, close to Hong Kong and Shenzhen, and are helping to complete nuclear stations in Liaoning. There are plans to build nuclear stations in other eastern provinces.

Nuclear activities are centred on Lop Nur in the arid north west, where an H-bomb was first exploded in 1967. More recently, Baotou, in Nei Mongol, has been involved in the research and production of nuclear materials, as has Lanzhou with its supplies of hydro-electric energy. In fact hi-tech research and ancillary developments are now widespread. Beijing scientists have created a low temperature district-heating nuclear reactor, while, on a larger scale, Shanghai constructs rockets for the space programme, and Xichang Space Centre in Sichuan launches satellites for telecommunication, meteorological and survey purposes.

In Focus ....

- Arguments for and against hydro-electricity, as opposed to fossil fuels, involve renewable as opposed to non-renewable sources, restrictions on location of plant, and initial cost of development. Examine the advantages and disadvantages of future large-scale HEP developments in China.

The Three Gorges Project

The Sanxia Dam project, creating the Three Gorges Reservoir and the world's largest HEP generating plant with 26 turbines, is about to be developed in three stages over 11 years. Apart from problems of funding and construction, many economic, social, ecological, and environmental issues are involved, and the project has caused a great deal of controversy.

Advantages

● A clean source of 18 million kw capacity will distribute energy through grid systems to supply the Chang jiang corridor and the proposed Sanxia SEZ, including eastern Sichuan.
● Controlled summer discharge will act to check flooding, especially over the adjacent, vulnerable Jianghan plain, and reduce silt accumulation in the reservoir. In winter clearer water will raise the storage level.
● In summer 11 500 tonne ships could reach Chongqing, and improved navigation downriver would reduce freight costs.
● The reservoir and adjacent cliffs would form an attractive landscape, and there would be fish breeding potential.
● Micro-climatic changes with slightly warmer winters would suit local orange growing.

Problems

● With the huge cost, the time lag, and the energy lost during distribution, smaller stations elsewhere might be preferable.
● Relocating over 1 million people, with new townships, enterprises and roads means social disruption at great cost.
● The necessity of farming steeper land because of relocation would lead to soil erosion.

● Submergence will destroy historic relics, and disturb wildlife habitats and fish-spawning sites. Tourism could decline with the disturbance of unique gorges.
● Construction will add eroded material to a reservoir which is already prone to siltation, as will slips from weak shales over soluble limestones.
● The rapid summer flow making contact with the relatively still backwater of the reservoir could cause deposition and siltation and affect navigation.
● The additional weight of the water may trigger earthquakes.
● A stronger, cleaner flow downstream could scour existing protective dykes.

The Facts

● Thermal plant of this capacity would burn 50 million tonnes of coal a year, with accompanying pollution.
● Nearly one-third of the budget is targeted for resettlement.
● Teams are working at historic sites to minimise loss and transfer relics.
● Tree planting will cover areas eroded by construction.
● Foreign firms are involved, making direct investments, but the anticipated cost is large and may increase over time.
● Geologists acknowledge that local fault slips are probable, but discount the likelihood of a major earthquake in this region.

In Focus ....

● Consider the advisability of creating a super-dam, when those built in other developing countries have revealed severe social disadvantages as well as benefits.

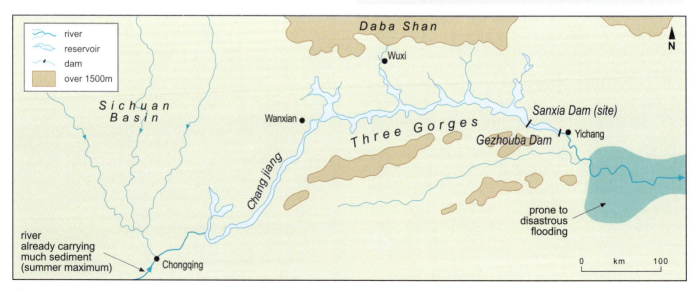

Figure 4.14 The Sanxia Dam site and the extent of the reservoir when the project is complete

China's regional diversity

PART 5

The North East (Manchuria)

From 1904-5 Manchuria, rich in coal, oil, metallic ores and with grasslands of agricultural potential, was targeted for exploitation and fought over by Russian and Japan. From then, until defeat in the 1939-45 war, Japan controlled the North East through assenting warlords, and after 1931 by direct occupation. Regarding it as a supply base, the Japanese opened up coalfields, developed iron and steel industries and shipped metal to Japan for manufacturing, together with foodstuffs for its increasing population. They also built an effective rail network.

Industrial concentrations

Factories and machinery devastated during the 1939-45 war were replaced, initially with the help of Russian plant and technicians, and so heavy industries expanded. From 1960 onwards oil and petro-chemicals have added to the economic strength of the North East. The heavy industries have remained largely under state control, with consequent restraints. Nevertheless the North East is now acquiring new manufacturing and commercial enterprises backed by foreign technology, investment and participation, especially by the Japanese.

Figure 5.2 shows the concentration of industrial cities in Liaoning, the southern province. **Anshan**, the main iron and steel manufacturing city now imports some ore but continues to receive coal from the North East, much of it mined near Fushan and Benxi, another steel producer. These industrial cities are almost satellites of the provincial capital **Shenyang**, the main commercial centre and rail focus. Shenyang has produced specialised machinery, machine tools and electrical equipment for a long time, but foreign investment is helping to widen its manufacturing base, which now includes aircraft, textiles and chemicals.

Dalian: the key port

Shenyang is linked by rail and a highway to **Dalian** on the Liaodong peninsula, the largest sea port in North East China with a tanker harbour and refinery which receive oil by pipeline from Daqing. Its industries include shipbuilding, engineering and textiles, but as an open coastal city courting foreign enterprises it has become part of an economic and technological development area, able to export competitive hi-tech products. The smaller ports of Yingkou, at the mouth of the Liao and Dandong on the lower Yalu River, also encourage foreign participation in manufacturing for export.

Dalian is located between the industrial-agricultural North East and the 'Bohai Economic Sphere' (page 58), close to Japan and Pacific shipping routes. It has an international airport and proposed land link to Shandong (page 81), and is likely to be a key centre in North East Asia's economic development.

Farmlands and industrial nuclei

The extensive north eastern 'plains' are a structural rolling lowland with a low watershed which separates the valleys of the shallow, silty Liao River and the navigable Sungari River. In the south the Liao lowland, with hot, moist summers, grows rice and cotton as well as kaoliang and maize. The Liaodong peninsula, noted for its apples, also rears silkworms, which were introduced by the many migrants from Shandong. However, northwards the growing season becomes shorter, the winters bitterly cold and here large mechanised state farms attracted migrant communities, who farmed the black-earth soils for wheat, maize, soya beans,

Figure 5.1 Anshan in Liaoning. The steelworks and heavy industries contribute to air pollution, still a problem in many of China's urban concentrations

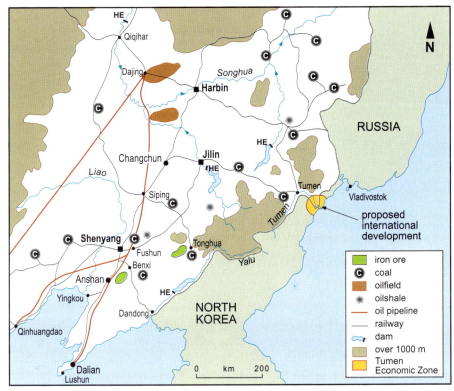

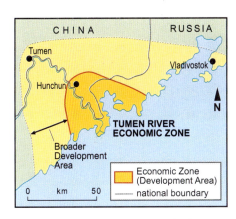

Figure 5.3 shows the proposed scheme to develop the Tumen River Basin through international co-operation

Figure 5.2 The North East with mineral resources, heavy industries and an outlet to Bohai attracts investment in modern manufacturing, especially from Japan.

sugar beet and oilseeds. Today, contract farming groups export maize and soya beans and supply the cities with grain, meat, and vegetables. This applies to the productive lowlands about **Changchun**, Jilin's provincial capital, which is China's largest vehicle manufacturer and now produces cars as well as trucks.

Eastward the province becomes more rugged, with the Changbai mountains attracting tourists. **Jilin city**, supplied by hydro-electric power from below a lake on the Songhua, produces fertilisers and petro-chemicals and distributes a range of chemical products within China and overseas.

The far North

Agriculture extends into Heilongjiang, which, despite a short growing season, also exports soya beans. Much of the north, including the Greater Hinggan mountains, has pine and larch forests, though over-felling and the extensive fires in 1987 have led to enforced conservation with replanting.

At **Dajing** hundreds of thousands are settled in a planned agro-industrial complex of communities, dispersed about the thousands of oil wells. Though past its peak production, the field is still China's largest oil producer, with pipelines running south to Dalian, Beijing and beyond.

Both Harbin and Qiqihar specialise in electrical equipment and machinery. **Harbin**, once a fishing village on the Songhua, is a city of over 3 million people,

manufacturing electrical equipment, turbo-generators, vehicles, chemicals and a host of consumer products. Around the city, on windswept reclaimed marsh protected by windbreaks, thousands of families grow fresh produce to supply to the city in summer, and process it for winter consumption, when the temperature often falls below -30°C.

There is a small but increasing, cross-border trade over the northern boundary, the Heilong River. The prospects of involving the north eastern provinces in the proposed international development of the Tumen River Area (Figure 5.4) have been considered, with Hunchun, the small river port, part of a Special Development Zone. The project, discussed as part of a UN Development Programme, would help China join Russia, North Korea, Mongolia, South Korea and Japan in establishing a North East Asian Development Area. While by no means definite as yet, this is nevertheless an indication of the growing economic power in the western Pacific.

In Focus ....

● As China emerges as a Pacific power, why are changes in international relationships likely to revitalise the north eastern provinces?

The economic influence of the Bohai Rim

More than 25 per cent of China's industrial output and exports are generated in a broad coastal region about the Bohai (gulf), the so-called Bohai rim. This economic zone of increasing prosperity includes southern Liaoning, the Beijing and Tianjin municipalities, and Hebei and Shandong provinces. However, its large manufacturing cities and industrial ports draw upon a wide area for energy and for materials for processing or direct export. This Bohai sphere of economic influence extends far inland, from southern Liaoning northward, and westward to parts of Shaanxi and Nei Mongol.

The coastal zone

Within the rim, ports are given priority for development, and as in the case of Dalian (page 56) have dual roles. Their location, site and rail connections enable them to serve the interior, while concessions to attract foreign investment both stimulate existing industries and introduce a range of new enterprises, often involving advanced technology. Thus **Qinhuangdao**, exporting oil from Dajing and coal from the far north of Shanxi province, has modernised its aluminium and glass industries with foreign assistance, and established a technological development area which attracts foreign engineering firms, notably from Japan and Australia.

On a larger scale, **Tianjin** (page 41), with express links to the capital and neighbouring provinces and a port serving a wide western hinterland, has acquired hundreds of foreign enterprises and leased land to large American and Japanese corporations. Together Beijing and Tianjin-Tanggu form a central concentration of economic power, flanked by the rapidly developing industrial regions in Liaoning and Shandong. Even the small port of Huanghua, developed to export coal from Shanxi, Shaanxi and Nei Mongol, is attracting engineering firms, and has acquired a chemical industry based on its existing saltworks.

On the Shandong peninsula, Yantai and Qingdao, original 'open ports', and Weihai with its hi-tech industries, are poised for expansion as direct links are established across the Gulf with Dalian and the nearby international airport is completed. Yantai has an investment area specifically for Taiwan and Hong Kong, while **Qingdao** has multiple interests in the Bohai economic boom as it exports coal and crude oil and has acquired hundreds of Sino-foreign firms. Qingdao has also introduced foreign technology to rejuvenate its textile manufacturing, based originally on cotton grown on the lowlands of western Shandong. These lowlands supplied grain to a brewery in Qingdao when it was a German treaty port and today the huge brewery bottles beer for nationwide distribution. Qingdao is also a tourist beach resort.

Away from the coast, **Shijiazhuang**, 280 km south of Beijing, developed amid a countryside of wheatfields and cotton, manufacturing textiles and tractors, but is now a major industrial city and a vital component of the Bohai rim. It produced China's first earth satellite station and encourages foreign investment in hi-tech research, biological engineering and electronic enterprises. The city also exports pharmaceutical products and refines oil from the Huabei field.

The sphere of influence

Shijiazhuang is a modern city with a spacious lay-out, but many cities in Shandong and along the Huang He valley are of ancient origin, with the remains of enclosing walls and industrial areas grafted onto a modified pattern of the old streets. Nevertheless, historic sites within or adjacent to

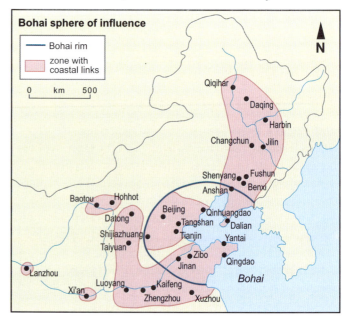

Figure 5.4 City ports about the gulf (Bohai) serve the adjacent economic rim and also wider zones with their own sources of energy and manufacturing concentrations

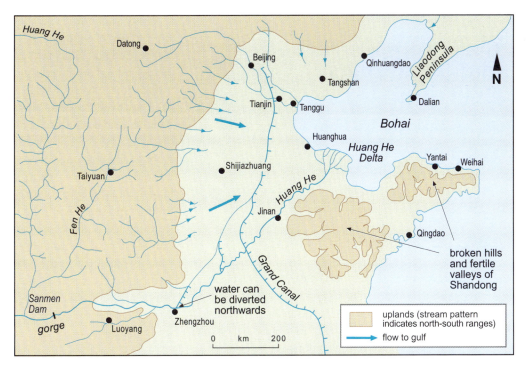

Figure 5.5 As China aims to strengthen its economic position in relation to its North East Pacific neighbours – Japan, South Korea, Taiwan, and Hong Kong – it encourages foreign investment in cities inland of the gulf (Bohai)

such cities provide a valuable, additional tourist income and this is certainly true of the former capital, **Luoyang**, situated on a southern tributary of the Huang He. Using energy from nearby coalfields, Luoyang became an industrial city manufacturing heavy machinery, tractors, mining equipment and chemicals. Today it has numerous foreign investment enterprises producing electronic and biotech commodities, but it is also a key tourist centre with many ancient temples, and is close to Longmen, whose remarkable examples of Buddhist culture are displayed in thousands of caves and grottoes (Figure 6.16, page 83).

The Fen River valley with adjacent sources of coal and iron ore plays a large part in the Bohai sphere of influence.

Figure 5.6 Growing affluence in the region is not only demonstrated by high-rise buildings and expressways, but by families like this with consumer goods: their camera, child's cycle, roller skates and casual clothes

Here **Taiyuan**, the capital of Shanxi, lies in a wide fertile basin surrounded by imperial and monastic remains, making tourism of growing importance. However, Taiyuan is primarily an industrial-commercial city (page 39), using local coal for steel and chemical industries and to provide thermal energy for manufacturing aluminium and textiles. Among more recently developed activities it monitors space satellites.

Further north, **Datong**, former capital of the Northern Wei, acts as a tourist base for visiting the Buddhist sculptures in caves at Yungang, 16 km to the west. It is a vital, if drab, manufacturing city, distributing coal, producing diesel and electric locomotives, and connected by electrified railway to the coast. In fact the influence of economic power in the Bohai rim extends even further inland. **Baotou**, the heavy industrial city in Nei Mongol, is linked by rail to Datong, and from here to the port of Qinghuangdao.

The whole 'sphere' has become part of the coastal zone development, and one aim is to encourage foreign economic relationships, in particular with China's Pacific neighbours and the USA.

In Focus ....

● Why do the economic relationships of 'port and hinterland' now apply to the broader coastal zone and sphere of influence of the Bohai rim? In particular, examine the roles of modern transport, communications and multinational interests.

The loess lands

Mobile but fertile

Much of Shaanxi south of the Great Wall, and parts of the adjoining provinces, are blanketed by accumulations of loess, several hundred metres thick. This is deeply dissected, due to summer storms acting on surfaces so soft that in time unpaved roads have been worn several metres below the surrounding countryside. Yet, as loess particles with a lime content readily adhere to each other, gulley sides remain surprisingly steep. In northern Shaanxi especially. families have created caves in loess slopes which provide them with a dry home that is warm in winter and cool in summer, its firm inner walls polished or plastered. Caves are also widely used for storage. The villages with earthen walls and unpaved roads appear part of the loess itself, their walls built by the traditional method of tamping earth between a vertical shuttering of horizontal poles (see Figure 2.16, page 27).

Figure 5.7 Low terraced fields with spring wheat extend over the loess north of Xian. Evidence of past prosperity is seen in the imperial tombs of the Tang dynasty which are great tourist attractions

Over the centuries people have terraced slopes for cultivation, but though carefully contoured they can become deeply gullied. Today millions of trees, mostly eucalypts, are being planted on hillsides to check erosion, and across wider valleys to act as windbreaks. Over the most populated areas, such as the flatter alluvial surfaces adjoining the Wei and Fen Rivers, young trees border fields and roads and enclose villages.

In northern Shaanxi the wheat is planted in spring, but further south winter wheat, millet, maize and cotton are grown on more stable arable land. About Xian, where a tributary to the Wei River supplies a canal system, the countryside is densely populated, with lines of pylons and cables crossing the landscape and electric pumps delivering water to channels in the light brown fields. Here families rear pigs under contract and treat their cabbages, onions, beans or spinach with chopped maize and pig manure – but use chemical fertiliser from local factories on the grain fields.

Figure 5.8 A river in the north east loess land indicates seasonal climatic variation. On its terrace a village, among newly planted trees, blends with the natural surroundings

Exploiting past and present

In **Xian** the street pattern, the old walls, and the large mosque which serves a sizeable Muslim population, reflect the past, although it is now an industrial city with a population of 3 million. Many of its textile factories use local cotton, and the steelworks supply industries associated with agriculture – making machine-tools, electric engines, pumps and fertilisers. However, it has also acquired aircraft and electronic industries and is a satellite monitoring and control centre, while numerous firms manufacture modern consumer products.

Coal comes from northern Shaanxi and electrical energy from the Sanmen Dam (page 52). Shaanxi also has a number of productive oilfields and large reserves of natural gas are being developed. The huge Fen valley coalfields in Shanxi,

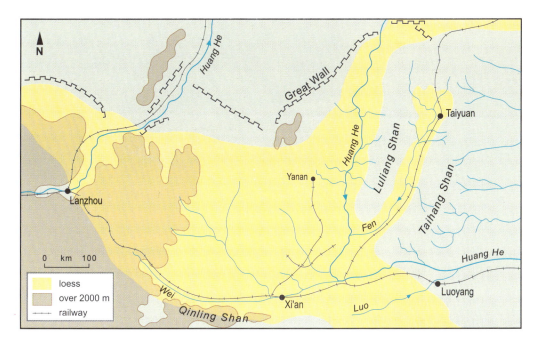

Figure 5.9 *(left)* The scale indicates the huge area covered by loess accumulations

Figure 5.10 *(below)* The village houses, shuttered walls and road seem part of the loess itself. There are young trees throughout the village and alongside its fields

and their importance to Taiyuan, Datong, and the Bohal rim generally, are considered on page 58.

Xian's ancient pagodas, which once housed Buddhist scriptures, have been restored, but it is the surrounding countryside which abounds with evidence of early imperial power and culture – the tomb of the first emperor, his remarkable terracotta army, and the clusters of outstanding tombs of the Tang dynasty (Figure 5.7). These, together with various temple sites, make Xian one of China's main tourist regions. More recent historic events are commemorated 270 km to the north at Yanan, which was the focus of the Communist society following the Long March.

A link between east and west

Eastward along the railway to **Lanzhou**, in eastern Gansu, the countryside becomes drier. Lanzhou, 1600 m above sea level in the narrow valley of the Huang He, has been a route centre since ancient times, and into this century received caravan traffic from the west. With the expanding rail network and energy from the Luijia Dam, Lanzhou has become an industrial city of economic importance to the developing north west. It now has research establishments and hi-tech industries associated with national projects, and is a centre of the nuclear industry. Lanzhou's oil refineries and petro-chemical complexes are linked by pipeline to western oilfields, and the additional railway line to Xinjiang helps it to serve the accelerating production in the far west. Lanzhou also manufactures aluminium, copper and various types of machinery. With a population of over 3 million it extends for 20 km along the southern bank of the Huang He. Although most factories are on the outskirts of the city,

pollution has continued to be a problem.

The rapid economic growth of Xian and Lanzhou is a response to Government targeting for accelerated development, and yet each of these provincial capitals owes much to a location which has, at various times in history, made it a dominant strategic city: Xian amid fertile, watered loess; Lanzhou a garrison settlement on a major trade route, now having important economic links with the west.

In Focus ....

- The fragile ecosystem of the loess lands has been disturbed over the ages. The whole region has an image of environmental degradation. However, this is only one aspect of the region. Consider the economic strengths of the area and describe the present advantages of its location between east and western China.

The Sichuan Basin

Figure 5.11 Canal water diverted from the Min River, channelled through mulberry trees

Sichuan ('four rivers') refers to the Min, Tuo, Jialing, and the latter's tributary the Fu River, draining southward to the Chiang jiang. The basin itself is enclosed by mountains: in the north the Min Shan; to the east massive limestones cleft by the Three Gorges; and in the west high parallel ranges bordering the great plateau. Much of the lower basin is a series of valleys and alluvial plains, separated by hills and underlain by soft red sandstones. Sichuan's richest agricultural region is the densely populated Chengdu plain, crossed by the Min jiang and numerous canals. Figure 5.12 shows the Min River diversions, first made in the third century BC, and the network of canals developed about Chengdu. Unfortunately, deforestation in the mountains is causing great erosion, more rapid runoff, and summer flooding in northern Sichuan, so that the Jialing River carries increasing loads of silt to the Chang jiang.

A favourable climate

The Sichuan Basin tends to be cloudy in winter; also mountain barriers shelter it from the cold north-westerlies,

and air warms as it sinks into the basin, allowing January temperatures to average some 10°C. In mid-summer, when the mean on the Chengdu lowland is 29°C, moist air from the south brings about 1000 mm of rain. Thus much of Sichuan, the largest province with about 100 million people, has a climate which favours agriculture and supports natural forests containing many unique plant and animal species.

The climate allows double-cropping, with rice following winter wheat in a matter of days, and suits a wide variety of crops, including sugar cane, maize, citrus and deciduous fruits, rape, sesame, soya beans, sweet potatoes, tobacco, cotton, tung and tea, all varying with altitude and location. Millions of mulberry trees planted in and about the fields and alongside roads and water courses supply the many silk factories, especially around Chengdu. In some regions oak leaves are fed to the silkworms.

Throughout Sichuan the drainage systems have influenced settlement patterns. Small townships occupy river terraces, and many of the larger towns have developed as route centres on waterways.

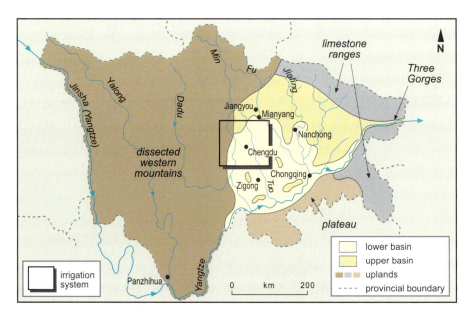

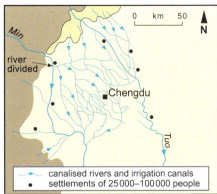

Figure 5.12 *(above)* The extensive irrigation system developed from early diversions of the Min River

Figure 5.13 *(left)* The Sichuan Basin, which includes (Figure 5.12) the extensive irrigation system developed from early diversions of the Min River

Energy and industrial development

The province has many sources of energy. Cities which originally depended solely on coal-burning power stations now receive gas from a number of fields within the basin, and oilfields lie south of Chongqing, where small HEP stations add to locally generated thermal energy. Zigong has chemical industries based on the extraction of both salt and gas, and there are productive oilfields near Nanchong in the Jialing valley.

The deep-cut, fast-flowing western rivers offer many potential sites for HEP generation, like that on the Dadu River (Figure 4.10, page 52). In the far south west, a hydro-electric power station is being built on the upper Yangtze (Jinsha River) close to **Panzhihua**, its steelworks sited in a rift valley rich in iron, vanadium and titanium. In less than 30 years it has become an industrial city of nearly 1 million people. To the south east is the site of the massive Three Gorges project, examined in some detail on pages 52-54.

Chongqing is the largest city in the basin and the industrial hub of south west China. Its core is a steep wedge of land between the Jialing and Chang jiang, with houses and factories extending alongside both rivers. Its role as a communications centre and transhipment port will be enhanced by the completion of Three Gorges Project.

War with Japan boosted Chongqing's manufacturing, for plant was brought from the east, while iron ore and coking coal to the south of the city supplied new steelworks. Today, apart from producing metals, machinery, textiles and chemicals, it has a technological development zone and hundreds of foreign-funded enterprises, such as the Sino-Japanese Yamaha firm producing motorcycles from parts produced locally.

Chengdu, the provincial capital with a flourishing commercial centre (page 39), is very much a regional city,

Figure 5.15 A village on the Min lowlands, wheat against white walls, rice in the field, lotus in the near pond and that beyond stocked with fish

part of a rich, irrigated, agricultural countryside, but is also industrial. Here again there are long-standing silk, metallurgical and chemical industries, but also considerable foreign involvement in firms using modern technology, especially those producing electronic apparatus such as computers.

In the north of the province two cities play special roles in China's technological-industrial development. **Mianyang** includes a 'science city' which researches and develops products such as instruments for space and radar equipment and ultra-sonic apparatus for medical use, and manufactures TVs on a production-line basis. In **Jiangyou** the province's main steel complex is noted for its high quality products suitable for aircraft, oil-rigs and other specific purposes.

Sichuan has been at the forefront of progress both in industry and agriculture. It pioneered the responsibility system; although unfortunately, as described on page 33, this has tended to increase rural unemployment. Large numbers from the rural areas have become migrant labourers, many of whom swell the floating population of the eastern cities.

Figure 5.14 Chongqing ferry terminal at the Jialing-Chang jiang confluence

In Focus ....

- Review the physical conditions and historical events which have combined to make the Sichuan Basin such a densely populated province.

- What positive and negative influences have Sichuan's western mountains had on the development of this part of China?

- Figure 6.12, page 81 shows part of the railway which links Chengdu and Kunming through these western mountains. Even this small sector with its bridge and tunnel indicates the immense cost of such complex projects. What might be the priorities for authorising such construction?

Yunnan: environment versus economic potential

Figure 5.17 A Yi minority village amid the forested mountains of southern Yunnan with rice in the valley and bananas on the slopes

A province of immense variety

In western Yunnan narrow mountain ranges separate steep, forested gorges of the upper Yangtze, Salween, Lancang and Yuan Rivers. To the east the plateau surface, at about 2000 m, is broken by rift valleys, some with deep lakes between fault scarps, and by river systems draining eastward and southward. It also has spectacular *karst* limestones.

Extensive forests in western and southern Yunnan have the greatest variety of plant and animal species in the country, though their preservation is at risk from projects to develop the south west economically. At the moment, however, the natural ruggedness and inaccessibility is sufficient to maintain the comparative independence of the numerous minority peoples, 26 ethnic groups, who make up one-third of the province's 40 million people. Most have their own customs, but many are comparatively poor, thus facing the problem of retaining independence while making use of opportunities. Some, like the Dai people in the south, are developing alongside the Han majority; while among the snow-capped ranges of the north west are progressive towns, such as Dali and Lijiang, centres for strong minorities whose ancestors commanded the south west gateway to India.

Recent development

Kunming, the provincial capital, on the edge of the fertile basin containing Lake Dian (Dian Chi), was founded as a walled city early in the nineteenth century. In 1908, in the knowledge that there were partly worked ores of copper, tin and other minerals in northern Yunnan, the French completed a railway from Indo-China to Kunming. The real expansion took place during war with Japan when refugees from the East poured into the city, and military and civilian supplies arrived along the Burma Road, and were later flown over 'the hump' from north east India. Kunming acquired a mixture of cultures as it attracted people from various parts of the province and later received numerous Vietnamese refugees. As there was no railway eastward to Guiyang until the late 1960s, the whole area retained its regional characteristics in relative isolation.

Today Kunming is an industrial focus for the south west, with railways through the western mountains to Chengdu and east to Nanning. There are steelworks and copper smelters nearby, with factories manufacturing machine-

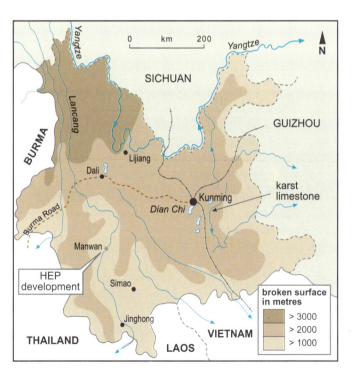

Figure 5.16 Yunnan Province. Notice the deep-cut valleys among the western mountains and the plateau broken by faulting and dissected by rivers flowing eastward to the Xi jiang and southward into Vietnam

Figure 5.18 Sani women beside a lake in dissected limestones, whose karst pinnacles are a tourist attraction

Figure 5.20 A fertile valley in eastern central Yunnan. Ploughing with water buffaloes prepares soils for a rice crop to follow the winter rape

tools, electrical equipment, chemicals and textiles spreading to the lake shores. However, Kunming has a spacious layout with landscaped parks, and its leafy suburbs with colleges and agricultural institutes extend into the hills. Intensively cultivated flats with a network of water channels and nucleated villages border the lake, and here too the winter wheat gives way to rice within a few days.

The climate has been described as 'eternal spring' with moderate temperatures (monthly means from 9°C to 22°C) and mid-summer rains, its sunniness emphasised by the provincial name Yunnan – 'south of the clouds' (of Sichuan). This favours a variety of crops. Wheat, rice, rape, sugar cane, tobacco and mangoes are grown around the villages; those in the broad structural valleys draw water from natural lakes and local reservoirs.

Figure 5.19 A machine-tool factory amid rice fields, where Kunming's industries spread westward along lowland bordering Dian Chi

Tourism is of growing importance in Yunnan province. Dian Chi is an impressive stretch of water 40 km long, bordered by farms, fishing villages and the spectacular fault-bounded Xi Shan (Western Hills) with their temples. Kunming is a base for visits to the many historic sites amid the nearby hills and the plateau beyond, to the limestone pinnacles at Shilin (Stone Forest) and to villages in the deep terraced *poljes* of the karst country. Small airports now make it easy to visit the Dai communities of Xishuangbanna in the far south, where the burden of the increasing population is threatening the rainforest.

Energy projects: likely effects

Thousands of small hydro-electric generators provide energy for the villages and market towns, and now five large hydro-electric stations are being built on the Lancang jiang to feed a regional power grid, with a dam at Xiaowan creating the main reservoir, 40 km upstream from Manwan.
The Manwan and Dachoshan stations are already operating and energy is becoming available for the development of other non-ferrous mineral resources such as phosphates, lead and zinc, with the help of foreign investment. There will also be easier access to the southern forests. These already yield rubber and timber, and with cacao and pepper being such valuable crops, this raises concern about the forests' preservation.

In Focus ....

● Consider the following in respect to the settlement pattern in Yunnan: relative accessibility; the extent to which distant political decisions have effected considerable changes; the justification for current policies which will disturb unique environments.

The heart of the Chang jiang corridor

In order to accelerate rural and industrial development along this 'economic corridor' there has to be investment. This needs to be directed towards agricultural and industrial enterprises, the infrastructure of harbours, transportation and flood control, and to generating sufficient energy to attract new enterprises, which means building more regional power stations. This development also involves developing the potential of those parts of adjoining provinces which are, in a sense tributaries to the riverside 'strip'.

The Chang jiang corridor forms a 'T' with the developing coastal area about Shanghai-Pudong and the delta cities (page 68). Projects on the upper river about Chongqing and Panzhihua are considered on page 63, but here the central parts of the corridor, between the Three Gorges and the deep-water ports on the estuary, are examined. This area includes fertile lowlands with large shallow lakes, much of which is vulnerable to flooding and in need of further measures to control seasonal water levels (page 54).

This subtropical lowland has summer rains and a long growing season, which allow multi-cropping by families or co-operative groups, usually combining rice with either wheat, maize, cotton, ramie, rape or soya beans, and, of course, keeping pigs, poultry and fish-farming. Particular regions favour tung, oranges or mulberries, with tea crops in the more rugged countryside. The combination varies regionally, with increasing emphasis on cotton and mulberries towards the delta.

Despite the widespread distribution of energy generated at the Gezhouba Dam, increasing demands of industrial machinery and domestic appliances leave many parts of the corridor short of energy: hence the need to invest in regional power stations. In region A in Figure 5.21 new hydro-electric stations on the tributary Qing River benefit cities such as **Shashi**. This former Japanese treaty port now attracts many joint-venture enterprises, e.g. Sino-Japanese production of refrigerators. In fact northern Hunan (region B) which is rich in ores of tungsten, antimony, lead, zinc and mercury, offers more favourable financial incentives than the coast, and has acquired foreign investment in mining, power stations and export industries. For example, **Changsha**, noted for its metallurgical products, now sends fashion garments to Japan, while **Yueyang**, the rapidly developing port on Dongting Lake, has a sister city in Japan, and foreign investment enables petro-chemical, tung oil and textile industries to extend along both the lake and river. As an ancient city in a mountain setting, it also invests in tourist facilities.

Wuhan, a river port with 7 million people around the confluence of the Han and Chang jiang (region C), is the key city for economic development in the corridor. Two bridges provide a 'U' traffic system linking Hanyang and Hankou, on either side of the Han River, with Wuchan across the main Chang jiang (Figure 5.22). Hankou has financial and commercial interests, while Wuchang has set up science/hi-tech research institutes, backed by a

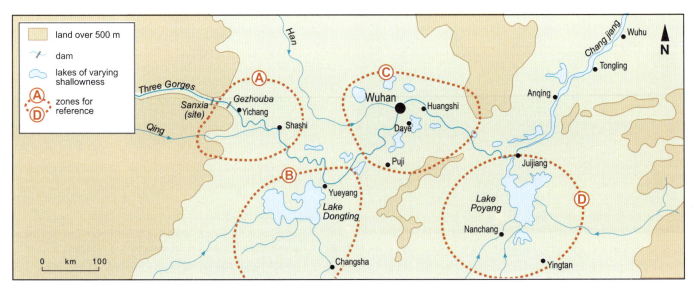

Figure 5.21 Economic development zones in the hinterland of targeted city ports along the transport artery of the Chang jiang

development zone where foreign investment helps to produce commodities such as fibre-optic cables and cars. The prospect of benefits from the Three Gorges project also attracts investors, who are helping to renovate lagging state-owned shipbuilding, machinery and textile industries. Downriver, a huge iron and steel complex obtains ores from Daye and coal from Puqi, to the south.

To the east of Wuhan the heavy industrial city, **Huangshi**, also obtains ores from Daye for steelworks which supply mills producing precision tools and tubing. Here, too, a new river bridge and enlarged harbour attract modern enterprises, including Sino-Japanese factories which, as part of a corporation with branches across China, produce and export Western-style clothing.

Jiujiang, at the foot of Mount Lu, one of the main rice ports on the river, has become another industrial route centre, serving an economic belt about Lake Poyang (region D). A bridge carries the Beijing–Kowloon railway across the river, and a new expressway follows the rail to **Nanchang**, the capital, which has aircraft industries and Japanese-funded vehicle factories. Jiujiang itself manufactures petro-chemicals and synthetic fibres, and processes copper from a mineral-rich hinterland, for **Yingtan**, east of the lake, is China's biggest copper smelter.

Yingtan is also a large fruit distributor, and Jiujiang markets tea, oilseeds, and fish. In fact Jiangxi is a rich agricultural province and, with attractive mountain scenery, encourages government-sponsored tourism.

The same development pattern is seen in Anhui province, where **Anqing** port has petro-chemical industries, produces synthetic fibres, and encourages investment in development zones, one of which is specifically funded by Taiwan. Further downriver, **Tongling**, with access to large mineral deposits, has enlisted foreign technology to increase its

Figure 5.23 The Chang jiang transports bulky goods far more economically than rail or road. These coal-barges supply riverside factories at Chongqing

production of copper and phosphate fertilisers, and is broadening its industrial base by offering preferential terms to foreign businesses.

Thus in each province there is a broadly similar response to the policy of spreading development from the coastlands and attracting economic growth around the previously established inland centres.

In Focus ....

- The plan of economic development based on the 'T' shape of the Chang jiang and coastal zone is very close to that of the Western powers during the late nineteenth century, when concentration focused on the 'treaty ports'. Why is this strategy now proving attractive internationally?

- River ports chosen as nuclei for the expansion of market zones have long been collection and distribution centres. Suggest why investment in harbour facilities and bridge building is now a priority.

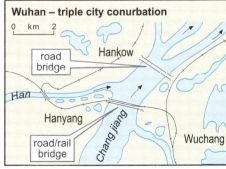

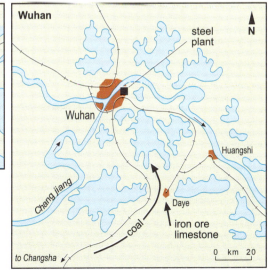

Figure 5.22 The conurbation of Wuhan, a centre of communication with the benefit of water transport and access to coal and iron ore

The Chang jiang estuary and coastal development

Figure 5.25 The densely populated industrial port of Shanghai, focus for both coastal and river corridor development

The estuary, delta lands and adjoining coastal areas form the core from which economic development is being expanded along the Chang jiang corridor. Many long-established centres of trade and industry, some former treaty ports such as Shanghai, Nanjing and Hangzhou, acquired an infrastructure related to European economic activities. Ancient and prosperous 'silk cities' like Suzhou, are now faced with establishing modern manufacturing while preserving their old pattern of canals, bridges, and gardens, both for aesthetic reasons and to encourage tourism.

Developing the lower estuary

As a rice-exporting port and rail junction on the lower estuary of the Chang jiang with textile and metallurgical industries, **Wuhu** was targeted for expansion. Container wharfs and preferential investment opportunities have helped to attract new enterprises, in particular Hong Kong companies manufacturing electrical apparatus for export to South East Asia. Further downstream, with coal, iron ore, and other minerals in the immediate vicinity, **Ma'anshan** developed a large steel complex, of prime regional importance until the completion of the Baoshan steelworks at Shanghai, and still highly productive.

Much of the corridor development is co-ordinated in **Nanjing**. Even though Nanjing has long been a key industrial and commercial city, it retains its traditional role as a cultural and educational centre, with broad avenues and ancient walls reflecting past prosperity. Its deep-water harbour with container wharfs can serve 30 000 tonne vessels, though transhipment is needed for upriver cargo. It receives and distributes coal and oil from the north, and has developed riverside steelworks, refineries and petro-chemical industries. Though many of its foreign-funded firms manufacture goods for export, it also specialises in research for hi-tech domestic industries, producing electrical appliances and telephone exchange systems. Today its long trans-river road and rail bridge is barely adequate, and another is planned.

Near the junctions of the Grand Canal and Chang jiang there are major water control schemes. A thermal power station at **Zhenjiang** provides energy to pump water from canal to river to prevent flooding, and back into the canal at times of drought. Across the river, near **Yangzhou**, another system can divert water northwards through the rich grain and cotton lands of northern Jiangsu, which from time to time have been devastated by flood or drought. **Xuzhou**, in northern Jiangsu, with its coal mines and heavy industries, is a route centre with railways to Lianyungang port, Beijing,

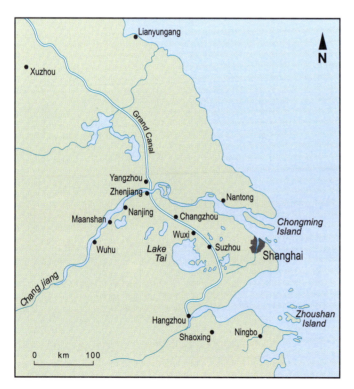

Figure 5.24 The Chang jiang estuary, delta, and coastal development zone, which include about one-sixth of China's population

Figure 5.26 The arc of industrial expansion in the agriculturally productive lakes region adjoining Shanghai

Figure 5.27 Barge traffic and industrial development along the Grand Canal in Suzhou. However parts of the city retain ancient characteristics and encourage considerable tourism

and the north west, thus providing a link with other developing areas.

On the lower estuary **Nantong**, a large port with shipbuilding and textile industries, has been hampered by cross-river ferry transport, but is to be connected to eastern Shanghai by a 5 km tunnel, and to Chongming Island by a bridge. Chongming itself supplies vegetables, meat and fish to Shanghai, and in anticipation of development similar to that in Pudong is constructing an ocean freight port and a bridge to Jiangsu, and has plans for a 25 km tunnel to Shanghai.

About Shanghai – an arc of expansion

West of Shanghai, in a landscape of lakes, rice fields, mulberries and canals, towns bordering Lake Tai like **Wuxi** and **Suzhou** were previously known for their silk and silken garments, and were a pleasant retreat for high officials. Today though, they too, are involved in general manufacturing. Suzhou retains its silk industries, but new enterprises of Japanese, Hong Kong, Taiwanese, South Korean, Dutch, Spanish and other foreign-funded firms produce a range of goods, from colour TVs to medicines. Within this arc around Shanghai many of the smaller towns, like Kunshan, have a host of manufacturing industries concentrated in specific zones.

Further south, Hangzhou, Ningbo, and Shaoxing have been trading centres since the seventh century, based on the

export of silk, brocade and satin. **Hangzhou** was a thriving capital under the Southern Song and, as a university city with a large lake in a hilly setting, has become a tourist centre. It is also, however, a major industrial city, with scientific research institutes, a hi-tech development zone, and much investment in export-oriented manufacturing, especially by the Taiwanese.

Ningbo is now a deep-water port and oil terminal, with thermal power stations and refineries encouraging Thai, American and Hong Kong companies to set up chemical and plastic industries. It is also developing an iron and steel complex, using imported raw materials. Even the offshore fishing is organised by Sino-Japanese companies, and Zhoushan Island exports frozen fish direct to Japan.

The emphasis here has been on foreign involvement in establishing industrial enterprises in a coastal development area, which receives energy from the Xinan Dam to the south, from the Qingshan nuclear plant, and from its own thermal power stations. However, this arc around Shanghai contains millions of families involved in producing rice, silk, tea and fish: while further north in Jiangsu the emphasis is on cotton, rice and wheat.

In Focus ....

- In China, past and present interact in many ways. Discuss how past events and modern economic activities are combined in the characteristics of the 'Silk Cities', the Grand Canal, and Inner Shanghai.

The South East: coastal dominance & inland potential

Figure 5.29 Spectacular karst limestone remnants reflected in the still, clear Li jiang

The western interior

In these subtropical and tropical parts of China there is a striking contrast between the rapid growth of *secondary* and *tertiary industries* in the coastal zone and the deprivation in the rugged interior of Guanxi and Guizhou provinces, with their mixture of ethnic groups. Difficult terrain and inadequate road and rail infrastructure have hampered development of the energy potential of these provinces and the use of their considerable reserves of phosphates, lead, mercury, zinc and aluminium. Investment is needed to complete the chain of power stations on the Hongshui (page 53), provide key road and rail routes between the cities, and improve navigation on the Xi jiang. The new Kunming–Nanning railway and the motorway between Nanning and Wuzhou will help to some extent.

In such terrain innovations tend to favour urban nuclei. Thus **Luizhou**, with additional energy for its metal industries, is acquiring new enterprises and tertiary occupations, but benefits for the many mountain villages and townships are less immediate. North of Guizhou, the spectacular scenery of karst limestone generates income from tourism centred on **Guilin**, which, with improved communications, now attracts secondary as well as tertiary industries.

Further south, **Nanning**, in a rich agricultural area, benefits from links with new coastal development about Beihai and Qinzhou in south eastern Guangxi, and from trade with Vietnam. Its department stores, selling TVs, electronic toys, and fashionable clothes, emphasise the emergence of an urban elite.

The coastal economic zone

Investments by Overseas Chinese with origins in the south east are extending the coastal development zone by establishing light industries at inland ports on the Xi jiang. For example, at Wuzhou and around Zhaoqing in hilly eastern Guangdong, and at ports downriver which trade with Hong Kong via the Xu jiang (Pearl River) estuary.

Guangzhou, 100 km up the estuary, has a long history of foreign commerce. In the 1850s Europeans, based on

Figure 5.28 The South East, where the coastal concentration of prospering cities contrasts with the rugged interior

Figure 5.30 A Yi family home in the forested western mountains

CHINA'S REGIONAL DIVERSITY

Shamian island within the city, re-exacted trading rights and established legations, banks, residences and commercial enterprises. However, as silting made the old port too shallow, docks were established 18 km down river at Huangpu, though even today siltation causes problems.

With some 6 million people, Guangzhou has spread far from the old CBD, and is developing a subway system. Amid the residential areas, with markets, stores and restaurants, numerous factories, mostly private enterprises, manufacture textiles, clothing, electronic goods and foodstuffs for both home consumption and export. Foreign investment has helped to create many thousands of new industrial projects and develop three technological development areas with new factories and high-rise blocks. These are located along the estuary, one of them close to the highway bridge which now links Shenzhen and Zhuhai.

About the city much of the intensively farmed land providing food and agricultural raw materials is owned by local entrepreneurs or rented to Hong Kong business people. Family farming has given way to intensive cultivation, often with hired labour. Many villages have become small factory towns, linked by an improving road network maintained by tolls. In towns like **Foshan** firms manufacturing clothing, pottery, toys and household commodities have a policy of recruiting young women, many of them migrants from distant provinces, some for short-term employment. Both Chinese and Hong Kong businesses find it cheaper here, and export the type of goods formerly mass-produced in Hong Kong itself. Again, the delta region is the ancestral home of millions of Overseas Chinese, many of whom finance local enterprises and help to obtain contracts abroad.

The rapid growth of the SEZs (page 44) means that after 1997 China's coastal south east region will form an

Figure 5.32 A bridge across the Xi River in Guangzhou. The people's concerns here are completely different from those of the family in Figure 5.30

enormous industrial–commercial–financial zone. It will be served by shipping using the estuary; by Hong Kong's harbour and new airport; by Guangzhou's airport; and by the combination of road, rail and water transport between Guangzhou, Hong Kong and the Special Economic Zones. To this must be added the developments taking place on Hainan Island (page 45), which, with its location, and the often independent outlook among its business communities, has become highly attractive to entrepreneurs dealing with foreign manufacturers.

Figure 5.33 New housing, indicating the profitability of intensive farming among these hills around Guangzhou and in the delta

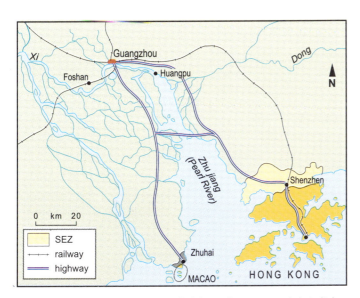

Figure 5.31 Guangzhou, the Xi delta and estuary, and their links with the SEZs and Hong Kong

In Focus ....

- Guangdong is becoming more financially independent, with more than 40 per cent of its industrial enterprises receiving foreign investment. Consider other historical, linguistic and locational factors which explain why Guangdong is looking for greater regional autonomy.

- Try to explain why state control has been relatively weak in southern China, and why 'clan' customs and festivities, formerly proscribed, have re-emerged in the interior, emphasising the gap between traditional and modern conditions.

The Arid Borderlands

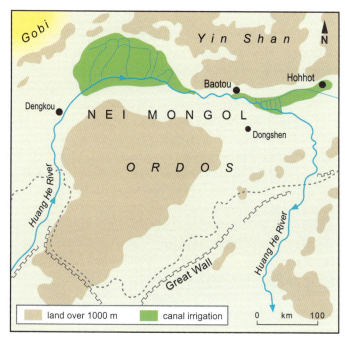

Figure 5.35 Irrigation along the Huang He, and the industrialisation of Baotou and Hohhot, have concentrated Nei Mongol's population in a relatively small area

Nei Mongol (inner Mongolia)

From the forested mountains of the north east, this Autonomous Region extends westwards across a plateau some thousand metres above sea level, becoming progressively drier towards the arid *Gobi* (waste), though much of it is steppe capable of supporting livestock herding.

Southwards the tableland rises to the Yin Shan ranges. These fall steeply towards the Huang He, where canal irrigation is used to produce spring wheat, oats, oilseeds, and sugar beet. Beyond the river, in the dry Ordos, north of the Great Wall, goats yield cashmere fibre for local textile factories at Dongshen and for export. Nearby coal mining districts supply Baotou and Hohhot, and the region is now developing its large reserves of natural gas. Nei Mongol is also developing sources of coal and oil in the north east and other minerals await exploitation.

Baotou, with over 1 million people, is a rapidly growing, heavy industrial city, producing steel and chemicals, and **Hohhot**, the capital, has added steelworks and an oil refinery to its older textile and sugar factories. Their urban populations are mainly Han Chinese, who form the majority of Nei Mongol's 22 million people. Today relatively few of

the 3 million Mongols are tribal *yurt*-dwelling, semi-nomadic pastoralists, for many of the better pastures are fenced off, and irrigation encourages settlement.

The arid north west

In Chinese central Asia snowy ranges skirt basins with deserts and oases. The scale is remarkable. The Tarim Basin, where the Taklimakan dune desert covers abundant reserves of oil and gas, is nearly 1300 km long and over 600 km at its widest. To the north the Tarim River runs though salt flats to saline Lake Nur. Streams fed by mountain snows build coarse alluvial fans before sinking into the sands, although

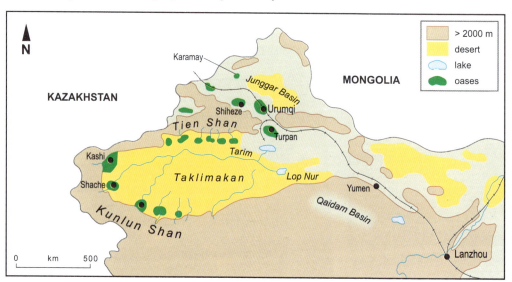

Figure 5.34 *(left)* Settlement in the far west is concentrated in and about sizeable towns, in basins, oases, and to some extent in oil-bearing localities. In-migration and investments in Urumqi have created a modern city aimed at 'opening' the north west

Figure 5.36 Urumqi, focus for development of the north west, enjoys an influx of investment for industries, roads, transport, and housing.

Figure 5.38 Shiheze, too, has new enterprises, including this tomato purée plant

there are irrigated oases whose settlements are linked by ancient routes. Towns like **Kashi** (Kashgar) became trading centres on the Silk Road. Its bazaars, mosques and ancient tombs now attract tourists, despite modern additions which highlight uneasy relationships between a large Uigur Muslim population and the dominant Han.

In basins to the north, canals, and groundwater brought from the mountains by underground *karez*, irrigate rice, wheat, sugar cane and particularly cotton, which tolerates slight salinity. Despite temperature extremes in the fault-bounded Turpan depression, the hot, sunny summers suit cotton, grapes and deciduous fruits.

North of the Tien Shan, with its spruce forests, it is less arid. Mountain slopes and the grasslands of the Junggar Basin support the flocks and herds of nomadic Kazakhs. Wheat and maize are grown in the Tien Shan foothills west of Urumji, and a network of canals irrigates extensive areas under cotton, sugar cane, oilseeds and tomatoes, all of which are processed in **Shiheze**.

This part of Xinjiang is rich in coal, oil and other minerals and the potential of the western oilfields is examined on page 51. **Urumqi** itself has acquired its large population mainly from the East and has come to resemble most eastern Chinese cities. It produces steel, machinery and oil products, and the hill country and irrigated farmlands supply raw materials for the manufacture of cashmere and cotton textiles and for processing sugar cane. Smaller enterprises now produce a variety of consumer goods. Improvements in the rail system will help to maintain its booming economy. Westward the railway joins the Russian system, while the long rail route to the east is now double-tracked.

Figure 5.37 Arid country south of the snowy Bogda Shan, with wind vanes supplying energy for settlement near Turpan

In Focus ....

● Consider the problems facing a strong minority group in a north western region of great economic potential, whose development will depend on an influx of technology and skilled personnel from eastern China.

Xizang, Tibet – concentration on Lhasa

The climate of Lhasa in the Gyi Qu valley, and in parts of the Zangbo valley, is milder than on the high plateau, though it ranges from 30°C in summer to below -20°C in winter. The growing season is only 140 days, but on restricted areas of arable land the Han Chinese have introduced suitable strains of winter wheat to replace highland barley, and also sugar beet, rape and a wider range of vegetables, as well as pigs and hardy cattle alongside the traditional sheep and goats. Tractors and harvesters are used on larger farms, mainly by the incoming Han Chinese, but tasks on family farms are mostly manual and there are still semi-nomadic herding families on the high plateau in yak-wool tents or small stone cottages.

Lhasa remains a remote city, and although there is a nearby airport, it is several days by road from Sichuan, Qinghai and the rail terminal at Golmud. It receives oil by pipeline from Golmud, and energy generated at two recently

completed hydro-electric stations. In Lhasa itself small factories or workshops produce processed foods, woollen textiles, footwear and farm implements. However there are virtually two cities, for while the western extension houses mainly Han Chinese, most Tibetans live in the old parts of the city, retaining their faith in Lamaism, the Tibetan form of Buddhism.

A number of monasteries destroyed during the Cultural Revolution have been restored, and the Potala Palace, residential focus of Lamaism, dominates the city. The scale of population movement from China to Tibet has created tension and incidents of unrest within the city. There are efforts to preserve the Tibetan language, but although the thousands of Tibetan teachers trained in eastern China may well produce a new literate generation of Tibetans, they will tend to steer them away from their past culture towards the broad ideals of the new China.

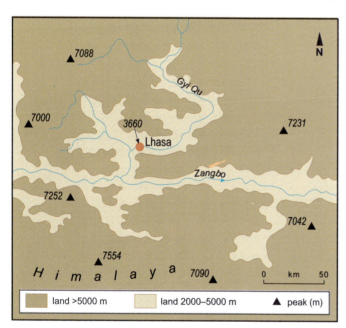

Figure 5.39 Lhasa in the remote Gyi Qi valley, tributary to the Zangbo (upper Brahmaputra)

Figure 5.40 Lhasa, with the Potala dominating the city. New buildings stretching along the Gyi Qu valley reflect the influx of Han Chinese

Rapid change with growing momentum

- The return of Hong Kong

- Increasing links with Taiwan

- Communications: priority for development

- Trade, investment and tourism

- The growth of rural enterprises

- Environmental problems

- Facing the future

PART 6

The return of Hong Kong

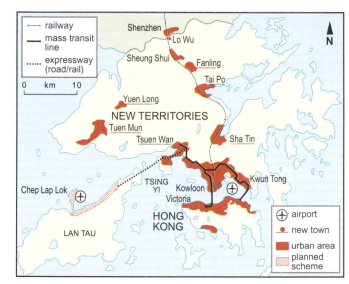

Figure 6.2 Hong Kong's Mass Transit Rail system between Victoria and the New Territories, with sites of the new airport and urban Lan Tau, and bridge links with Kowloon

Britain acquired Hong Kong's rocky island of weathered granite by Treaty in 1842, and in 1861 China ceded the peninsula of Kowloon to Britain. In 1898 a 99-year lease of the New Territories and various islands provided farmland, villages, and fresh water supplies. The first settlement, Victoria, now spreads from a high-rise financial–commercial centre along the north coast of the island, while across the harbour millions live in Kowloon and the expanding towns of the New Territories.

When the Japanese invaded in 1941, Hong Kong was a free port and flourishing commercial centre. After the 1939–45 War light manufacturing was encouraged, and numerous factories, workshops and craftsmen turned out textiles, garments and small artifacts. Over the years, with a trade recovery embracing the western Pacific, Victoria and Kowloon acquired high-rise offices, hotels, and shops packed with consumer goods – cameras, watches, electronic apparatus and clothes. Above all, Hong Kong became a major global financial centre.

China has found Hong Kong to be an important commercial outlet and has acquired interests in its stores, banks, insurance firms and real estate. Conversely, with China's *open policy*, Hong Kong businesses invest in the PRC, taking advantage of low wages, cheap land and tax concessions to set up tens of thousands of companies in Shenzhen and elsewhere in Guangdong, employing millions of workers. They are also aware of Guangdong's potential as a consumer market. As these mainland factories produce cheap clothes, plastic toys and domestic products, Hong Kong's own workforce has moved towards higher-value activities.

With over 6 million people in Hong Kong, there is pressure on living space, water supplies, sanitation and employment. Hong Kong has provided a haven for refugees

Figure 6.1 Hong Kong: the harbour; high-rise Victoria; and The Peak

Figure 6.3 Vegetable shops selling mainland produce

Figure 6.5 *(above)* An array of new high-rise flats extends eastwards from central Victoria along the harbour

Figure 6.4 *(left)* A Kowloon side street illustrates the intensity of commercial activity in Hong Kong

from South East Asia and has been a magnet to mainland Chinese, especially for those in Guangdong, attracted by remittances from relatives in Hong Kong and by TV images. Since the mid-1960s it has received over 1 million illegal immigrants.

Central land values in Hong Kong are extremely high. The older streets are crammed with stores, workshops, small offices and crowded living quarters. Beyond there is packed, speculative real estate, with a multitude of high-rise flats fringing the harbour.

In the New Territories there are both expanded market towns and industrial New Towns, with cross-shaped blocks of flats each housing up to 8000 people, many of whom commute to work in the centre. Each New Town tends to be associated with specific activities: Tsuen Wan, for example, with the nearby container terminal and local textile and chemical factories; and Tuen Mun with its adjoining heavy industries. Industrial towns lie along the electrified railway through the New Territories to Shenzhen, and from 1997 will be part of a continuous economic–industrial corridor in south east China. Intensive cultivation in the New Territories can produce up to eight vegetable crops a year, but even so Hong Kong draws on The People's Republic for fresh food, additional electricity, and extra water piped from the Dong jiang.

With hundreds of thousands commuting daily, the city centre is served by cross-harbour ferries, road tunnels and the underground Mass Transit Railway (MTR), which extends into the New Territories.

The international Kai Tak airport, stretching from the peninsula into the harbour, is being replaced by a new airport, extending from northern Lan Tau across the enlarged Chep Lap Kok island. A linear city with a population of 200 000 will be developed along northern Lan Tau, with an expressway and high-speed railway running for 35 km from the airport, across a 2.2 km suspension bridge, to central Hong Kong. There will be a third cross-harbour tunnel from west Kowloon.

The sheltered harbour, with berths for almost 100 vessels, has numerous container terminals. One, Kwai Chung, handles over half the cargo. Rapid hover-ferries serve Shenzhen, Macao and Zhuhai.

Most of Hong Kong's imports come from China, Japan, Taiwan, the USA and Singapore. Those from China reflect the operation of Hong Kong firms in Guangdong; for while Hong Kong receives over 40 per cent of China's exports, 25 per cent of its re-exports return to China as materials for processing and the finished products are then shipped abroad. Other re-exports go mainly to the USA, Japan, Taiwan and South Korea. Of Hong Kong's exports, China and the USA each take about 25 per cent, followed by Germany, the UK, Japan and Singapore.

In 1997 Hong Kong becomes a Special Administrative Region, Xiangang, within the People's Republic. China has agreed to a continuation of Hong Kong's social, economic, legal and other systems for at least 50 years from that time, and so Hong Kong should enjoy a high level of autonomy, although this does not extend to its foreign affairs and defence. China will benefit by maintaining the island's role as a free port and independent tariff area, and from its international banking status.

In Focus ....

- Look at and discuss:
  a) the advantages to China of admitting Hong Kong to a southern grouping of 'million cities' which includes Guangzhou, Shenzhen, and Zhuhai;
  b) the disadvantage of administering a 'megalopolis' of this size from Beijing.

- Explain why the benefits which Hong Kong businesses enjoy in producing light consumer goods on the Chinese mainland are likely to continue.

Increasing links with Taiwan

Taiwan, 160 km from the Fujian coast, is an island of east–west contrasts. Forested mountain ranges running parallel to the east coast give way to deforested, badly eroded hill country in the west. Beyond this a densely populated alluvial plain supports rice growing, a winter catch-crop, and profitable exports of sugar, bananas, and now canned asparagus and mushrooms. Of Taiwan's 22 million people, more than 6 million live in the capital, Taibei (Taipei), and nearly 2 million in the main port of Gaoxiong (Kaohsiung) in the south west.

Chinese colonised the island under the Ming, when Portuguese named it *Ilha Formosa* (beautiful island). Since then it has twice received a sudden influx of mainland Chinese. The Manchu invasion in the seventeenth century caused nearly 2 million to flee to Taiwan, though it shortly became part of Fujian province. The Japanese then seized the island in 1895, but were removed in 1945; and from 1949 over 1million Chinese Nationalists settled there under Chiang Kai-Shek, calling it the Taiwanese Republic of China. Today, as Taiwan, a capitalist society with rising living standards, the concept of providing rulers for mainland China is less attractive to a younger generation involved in rapid economic progress.

Hi-tech industrial output

Until 1965 the USA provided almost all the financial help for Taiwan, but now there is widespread foreign investment in development projects. Early land distribution schemes and co-operative ventures mostly failed, mainly because of their small size and lack of capital. As opportunities in manufacturing increased many left the land, and larger farming projects were introduced, using better techniques and planned irrigation. However, with booming industries and an increasing urban population, Taiwan now imports almost half its food requirements.

Initially, light industries were encouraged and with plentiful labour, long hours of work in small workshops and foreign investment in factories, Taiwanese textiles, footwear and toys began to compete on world markets. Today there is competition for cheap goods from other parts of Asia, so the emphasis is changing to more expensive products, and Taiwan's hi-tech industries are finding a world market. Industrial districts, most of them linked by the west coast highway, produce metals, machine parts, diesel engines and

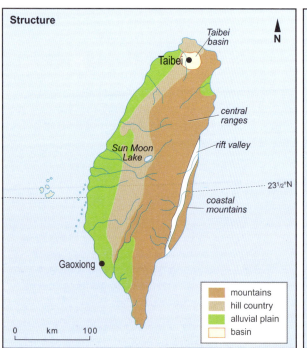

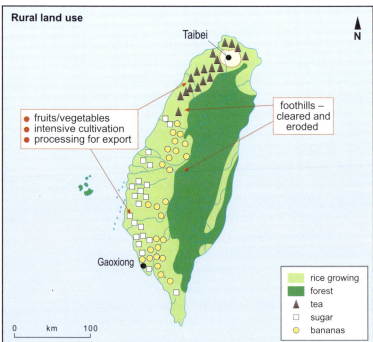

Figure 6.6 *(left)* The structure of Taiwan, with a rift valley among the mountains, heavily eroded foothills to the east, and a corresponding distribution of rural land use **Figure 6.7** *(right)* Intensive farming now dominates parts of the western coastland

Figure 6.8 Taibei's telecommunications centre in a district specialising in electronic industries

electronic apparatus. Xinzhu has an Industrial Park with over 100 firms specialising in computers and telecommunications, and is creating a Science City. Energy is supplied by hydro-electric plant near Sun Moon Lake in the central ranges, by thermal stations using natural gas, and by nuclear reactors.

Petro-chemicals and steel are among Taiwan's biggest industries. **Gaoxing**, a bustling industrial city-port choked with traffic, has refineries, petro-chemical and aluminium plants and shipyards. The northern port Jilong (Chilung) also builds tankers and bulk carriers.

Taibei is a sprawling, expanding city; its central districts with stores and offices are crowded with motor cycles, scooters, taxis and cars; its side streets loudly advertise shops and supermarkets. Beyond, a few older districts retain open-air markets, food stalls and one-room workshops, though many now have hotels, restaurants, and clubs. The influx of foreign interests and investment has not only produced advanced industrial enterprises (Figure 6.8) but an affluent section of society with a demand for recreational activities. Unemployment in the country as a whole is low, with a labour shortage, especially for low paid jobs.

China – Taiwan: mutual relationships

There is now increasing 'unofficial' trade between Taiwan and China, conducted largely through Hong Kong but also through Singapore and other countries with large Chinese populations. Taiwan has a big trade surplus with China, exporting industrial raw materials and spare parts and importing mainly agricultural products.

Thousands of Taiwanese firms invest on the mainland, where labour is plentiful and costs are less, setting up light industries. They are involved in many projects in Fujian

Province, where Taiwanese investment has stimulated the growth of Xiamen SEZ, and also in Hangzhou, Shanghai and parts of Guangdong. The PRC has created special zones for Overseas Chinese investment, encouraging, for example, Taiwanese interest in Meizhou Island, north of Xiamen, and at Yantai in Shandong, even though there is still officially no mutual recognition. It may well be that after 1997 the strong South China–Taiwan–Hong Kong linkage will encourage greater integration.

A growing number of Overseas Chinese from South East Asia, and from Chinese communities in 'Western' countries, have been returning to settle as wealthy entrepreneurs in Guangdong and Fujian. The Singapore Chinese have increasingly invested in hi-tech projects, especially in Hainan and the Chang jiang delta.

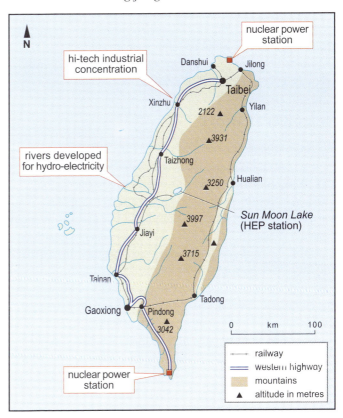

Figure 6.9 Taiwan's relief influences the pattern of communications and industrial location

In Focus ....

- Consider why, even though political tensions remain, is Taiwan's growing economic involvement with mainland China is to their mutual advantage.

- Account for Taiwan's huge investments in technical research institutes even though most firms are of small or medium size.

Communications: priorities for development

The development of modern communications in China has been hampered not only by the country's size and topography, with the eastward flow of large rivers separated by rugged country, but also by the late adoption of transport technology, by the initial concentration on foreign-dominated economic centres, by under-funding and, until recently, by a lack of foreign investment.

Water transport

The inhospitable nature of western China has acted to isolate communities in locally favourable habitats. In the east, water transport offered an alternative to the use of animals, and from early times canals linked navigable streams, rivers and lakes. The need to move grain stimulated canal construction as early as 130 BC, when a channel was cut from the capital, Chang-an, to the Huang He, bypassing the River Wei. By 600 AD the Sui had canal links capable of carrying rice from the Chang jiang lowlands to Luoyang and the Huang He. During the thirteenth century the Mongols extended parts of this system to complete the 1800 km Grand Canal from Hangzhou to Beijing. Much of this fell into disuse, but dredging, widening and lock improvements

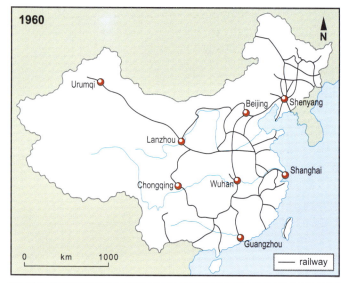

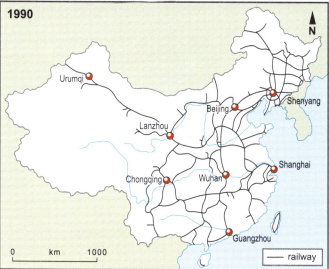

Figure 6.11 *(above)* Development of the railway system has speeded up in recent years with electrification and double-tracking, yet rail transport is still overcrowded and inadequate

now allow the south eastern stretches to carry rural commodities, coal and manufactured goods, and also to transfer water for irrigation. In the Chang jiang delta the age-old network of feeder canals is similarly adapted to serve the increasing flow of commodities.

The great rivers act as transport routes, though frequent flooding and the difficulty of bridging them have hampered long distance north–south travel. The Chang jiang is the most important artery, though seasonal variations restrict the size of shipping. The draught at Wuhan is 9 m in summer but only 2 m in winter, while upriver Chongqing must wait for the eventual completion of the Three Gorges

Figure 6.10 *(left)* Ferry transport across the Xi jiang, upriver of Guangzhou, with a bridge under construction

Project to receive shipping of a greater capacity. Nevertheless water transport greatly contributes to industrial development in the Chang jiang estuary and along the river 'corridor'.

Investing in the railways

The development of the Chang jiang corridor and its industrial ports is stimulating the creation of more road and rail bridges. Trains were ferried over the Chang jiang until 1956, when it was first bridged at Wuhan, then at Chongqing, and in 1968 at Nanjing. There are now some 12 bridges at the river cities, and plans for at least as many more. A new bridge for the growing industrial city of Jiujiang (page 67) will carry the new 2500 km north–south rail link between Beijing and Kowloon.

The shortage of long-distance road transport means that railways are immensely important, especially as links between industrial regions, and in encouraging economic development in the more remote parts of the country. Initially, most railways were built with foreign capital – those in the economically important north east mainly with money from Japan and the USSR. Despite the extension of the network shown in Figure 6.11, rail freight transport is still inadequate and public trains are overcrowded. This means that heavy investment is needed in rail construction, double-tracking, electrification, and manufacturing or importing engines and rolling stock. Figure 6.11 shows the absence of railways in the west, the isolation of Kunming, and the gap east of Wuhan, which has no direct rail link with the delta.

Joint communication projects

A number of extensive road and rail projects are evidence of China's ambition to create strong economic zones central to the North East Asian growth region. Within the Bohai rim (page 58) a joint development project aims to connect the Shandong and Liaoning peninsulas – by train ferry from Yantai to Dalian, and by combined bridge and tunnel across the Bohai Gulf between Pinglai and Lushun. This will require immense investment.

Expressways within and between major industrial cities, and as part of the infrastructure of development zones, are already increasing the economic strength of the eastern provinces. There is also more road building, of varying quality, in less developed parts of the country, focusing mainly on regional centres. But, once again, the size of the country and the need to attract investment for so many projects makes for targeting economically profitable areas, where the construction of roads, railways and airports will produce a suitable return.

Figure 6.12 The line through the western mountains between Kunming and Chengdu. Numerous bridges over the gorges and the many long tunnels point to the great investment needed to expand China's railway system and benefit the more remote communities

Tourism, now a considerable asset, is helped by improving access to scenic attractions, such as the karst country about Guilin, which has a modernised airport, and to historic sites, like the Buried Army near Xian.

The speed of economic reform means that many facets of communication have to be tackled simultaneously. Apart from the above, there are investments in satellite communication technology and the installation and nationwide linkage of telephone networks, with fibre-optic cables between selected areas. The need to concentrate on selected economic areas again highlights the problems of overcoming regional disparities.

In Focus ....

- The increasing affluence and greater mobility of China's population adds to pressure on the railway system. Explain China's difficulties of expanding the network to serve greater numbers more efficiently.

- Statistics show that, compared with coastal shipping, the cost of freight transport per kilometre is twice as much for river transport, three times for rail, and ten times for long-distance road transport. What are the implications of this for the economic development of the 'T' of the Chang jiang coastal zone?

- Coal makes up about one-third of freight carried (tonne-km). It is suggested that increasing consumption of oil and gas might lower this proportion. Why is this doubtful in view of the location of energy sources and coal's many uses?

Trade, investment, and tourism

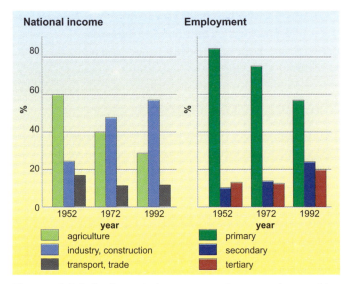

Figure 6.14 A relative decline in income from agriculture and in employment in primary industry is accompanied by a corresponding gain in income and employment in other occupations

In recent years China's international trade has increased dramatically. Between 1988 and 1993 the trade contribution to the gross domestic product (GDP) rose from 10 to 37 per cent. Also the nature of China's trade has changed, with increasing imports of machinery and transport, and exports of manufactured goods. Up to the 1970s natural resources – agricultural products and minerals – made up about 50 per cent of the exports. But in 1994 manufactured goods accounted for 80 per cent of the export earnings. Figure 6.14 shows corresponding changes in employment and relative contributions to national income.

Huge amounts of foreign capital have flowed in, both as investments and loans. With the attractions of a low-cost labour force, favourable tax concessions, a rapidly growing economy and a huge potential market, much of that has been in the form of direct investment. China's export earnings from joint ventures and foreign-owned enterprises rose from 5 per cent of the total in 1988 to over 20 per cent in 1992. In certain coastal areas foreign investors are able to purchase land for industrial projects, and may now produce for a Chinese market able to purchase foreign consumer goods.

The balance of trade has fluctuated. Formerly, imports were regulated according to receipts of foreign exchange. During the 1980s, after de-regulation, the large volume of imports needed to achieve rapid modernisation led to trade deficits. However during the early 1990s, as the volume of trade increased, the value of exports exceeded that of imports. But by the mid-1990s, a booming economy with huge capital investments was accompanied by increasing imports of processing equipment, vehicles, aircraft and consumer goods, and also a trade deficit.

Figure 6.13 shows the changes in the nature of exports and imports. Since 1980, when petroleum and its related products accounted for nearly 25 per cent of export earnings, oil exports have fallen sharply. In recent years clothing, textile yarn, fabrics and footwear have made up

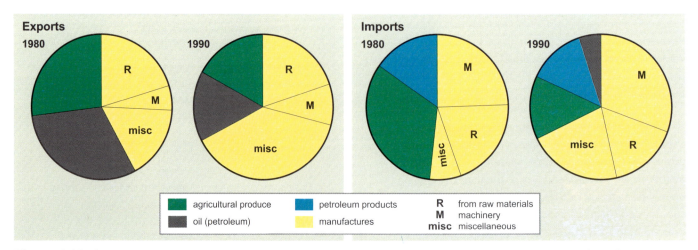

Figure 6.13 A comparison of both imports and exports over a decade, showing the significant effects of increasing industrialisation, construction work, and energy consumption

Figure 6.15 The spectacular rise in direct investment following the adoption of an open market policy with foreign involvement

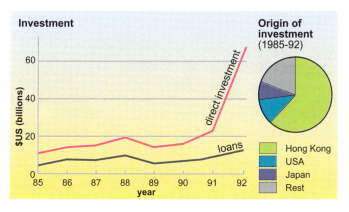

Figure 6.16 Buddha's supporting figures in the huge open-fronted cave at Longmen, near Luoyang, one of China's major tourist attractions. Here there is minor sales activity and interference with the statuary: both are undesirable features of tourist concentration

about 40 per cent of exports, accompanied by a variety of light consumer products. Many of these are processed from materials and goods imported by foreign-funded enterprises. When exported they earn about 20 per cent more than the cost of the imports. However, exports of electronic products and machinery, such as hydro-electric equipment, have also increased, particularly to other Asian countries and to developing countries in general.

Figure 6.13 shows the broad categories of imports, and the prominence of machinery (including forms of transport) related to current development projects. Of individual items, steel, needed for construction, and chemicals, especially fertilisers, remain major imports. Wheat imports fluctuate in volume according to home harvests, though increasing demands and a slow down in grain production suggest that these will remain high.

The rate of economic growth has been remarkable, averaging 9 per cent over the last decade. But with this has come **inflation**, rising to over 20 per cent in the mid-1990s, a figure which can lead to social unrest (in fact the response to soaring inflation led to serious public demonstrations in 1989). The 1990s inflation was due initially to adjusting commodity prices, which subsidies had kept almost constant under the commune system, especially those of foodstuffs. But recently the problem has related to over-spending and continuing subsidies for state-owned, inefficient industries, which continued to account for 40 per cent of industrial output. There are, of course, social problems involved in trimming a workforce while unemployment is large and increasing.

There are also important decisions to be made regarding the inflow of foreign capital. There is a great difference between loans from foreign countries and the World Bank and direct foreign investment, involving no repayment but from which the investor will expect a good return. Figure 6.15 shows the recent increase in direct investment, notably through Hong Kong, its subsidiaries in Japan, the USA, and Germany, and other eastern Asian countries.

Tourism

Loans and interest must be repaid, so China needs to recruit every possible source of foreign income. Here tourism has a role to play. There has to be investment in promoting China and in the necessary infrastructure to support tourism, such as hotels, transport and access to sites, though here, too, foreign firms can be involved. Such inputs will obviously continue to be necessary as tourism expands. Already many millions of tourists are arriving, attracted by China's landscapes, unique cultural heritage and historic sites. An additional incentive is the fact that until recently much of the country has been inaccessible.

As always with tourism, there are disadvantages. Because of the size of China and the abundance and spread of historic relics and scenic areas, there are relatively few instances of physical erosion by tourists. Nevertheless, focusing on a particular sites, such as the Great Wall at Badaling and the Terracotta Army creates an artificial local environment. Not only does this raise the possibility of degradation and pollution, but the tourists make contact with pedlars and profit-seeking entrepreneurs rather than with the local communities. Any spin-off for local people is usually concentrated on the site, perhaps involving displays of colourful local customs by organised groups, but it has a limited economic spread effect.

In Focus ....

● China's debts may be kept down by direct investments by foreign sources, but these are at the risk of the investor, and if profits are not realised this source will dry up. How might the need for such investments affect China's relationships with other countries, and also its policies at home?

The growth of rural enterprises

Figure 6.18 Many rural people now set up small enterprises in the townships, like this group selling medicinal products

Rural enterprises

As we have seen, the change from the commune system to families farming leased land for a contracted period, and to cultivation by co-operative groups, caused many to move away from traditional agriculture. Numerous small enterprises have been set up, owned collectively by villages and townships or run privately. The rural workforce can include the young (Figure 6.17) and the elderly, whose contributions are added to the family income and account for a general rise in living standards (although the opportunities for young people to be profitably employed has acted against even the modified one-child policy).

Some enterprises are small-scale and opportunist, for example kerb-side selling (Figure 6.18). Others are small-scale but well-organised, like the group of women providing textile materials and make-and-mend services from an established site (Figure 6.19), and paying taxes accordingly. Many small enterprises are in the form of workshops which

manufacture farm tools and equipment, sold locally on the open market. There are also small shops, street libraries and other service establishments in townships, and businesses in private hands which train and employ a number of people.

On a larger scale, many non-agricultural enterprises, with a varying number of employees, have obtained loans to set up factories processing local raw materials, or manufacturing clothes, household goods or building materials. By 1984 *township* and *village collective enterprises* were employing 40 million people and private enterprises 36 million. By 1990 rural collective and private concerns were each employing 47 million, and today over 100 million people work in such enterprises.

Not all have been well-run, or beneficial. In the early 1990s steps were taken to check the huge amount of credit provided by the Agricultural Bank and rural credit co-operatives, and to monitor the quality of products, many of which were deemed sub-standard. Attempts have been made to single out the most efficient enterprises for particular credit support, especially those producing export goods or working on contracts with larger factories. In theory, credit is being withheld from industries creating forms of pollution, but this is not always enforced.

Regional disparities

Production based on sub-contracting to larger manufacturers makes for higher efficiency and profitability. Enterprises most likely to do this successfully are those located near large towns and cities where communications are well-established and raw materials and products can pass freely between the main firm and sub-contractors. Thus

Figure 6.17 *(left)* Young people selling on the market bring in extra income – an incentive to have a larger family

Figure 6.19 *(left)* The increase in local spending power and changes in fashion mean thriving business for a group of girls renting a site in a Chengdu Street for making-and-mending

Figure 6.20 *(right)* This small collective group, given three tax-free years, set up a factory in Wuhan to make polyester textiles, bought new equipment within four years, and now manufacture for export

small factories can manufacture specific metal products of, say, aluminium or rolled steel, or can assemble precise electronic equipment.

For the mid-western provinces, and others in the interior with a less developed urban network, it is much more difficult for surplus labour to find employment in this way. The policy has been to boost economic activities in small and medium-sized provincial towns to counter rural unemployment and long distance migration; but this has been hampered by the sheer scale of the developments needed, and by local inertia or mismanagement. The employment of surplus labour for building better roads, housing, improving sewerage or providing cultural services is sometimes regarded by local administrators as 'non productive'. Existing industries have been required to give a small percentage of their profits to local public utilities, but in many cases their input has been used for other purposes, and with practices varying from town to town it is difficult to enforce an overall employment policy among dispersed rural communities.

On the positive side, the growth of rural enterprises has provided light goods, which are difficult to obtain from a large urban market, and has given employment to many millions, while the more favourably located have become part of the wider private manufacturing which is replacing many inefficient state-run industries. Overall rural enterprises have raised rural living standards, and so created demands for commodities formerly beyond the reach of village communities, encouraging further manufacturing.

On the negative side, apart from regional disparities, there are problems of pollution and mismanagement, while the loss of rural land together with increasing mechanisation to raise agricultural productivity, means that even fewer are needed on the land.

In Focus ....

● 'Population is the central issue'. Consider how this statement is relevant to most of China's problems, and how it affects the establishment of rural industries.

● Many factories in the state sector still run at a loss, giving priority to welfare rather than efficiency. A high proportion of the overall profits from industry is used to bail them out. In view of growing unemployment, examine the justification for such a policy.

● In Beijing alone thousands of new arrivals are registered as 'housemaids', and 'entertainers'. Liberalisation and changing aspects of urban social life add to the 'pull effect' for job-seeking migrants. Consider the problems of administration.

Figure 6.21 With new building in villages and townships, local brick-making has become a profitable enterprise

Environmental problems

China has numerous environmental problems, though again it is dangerous to generalise when much of rural China is still productive farmland, created by traditional skills in water management, terracing, and the use of natural fertilisers. Much of the barren territory is due to natural conditions, and the term 'desertified' is apt to be misused in relation to the huge arid and semi-arid areas in the west. Nevertheless, considerable areas of severe erosion are the result of disturbing a fragile ecosystem over the centuries, as in the loess lands.

Undoubtedly environmental problems have become more serious since the foundation of the PRC, partly because the population has more than doubled, partly through neglect during the Cultural Revolution, and partly through self-excuse knowing that most of the developed world has gone through a phase of 'pollute first, clear up later'.

Side-effects of rapid development

During the last two decades there have been great efforts to counter environmental degradation in China through practical projects, such as afforestation, with local government enlisting popular support for protective measures. Unfortunately poverty, combined with a lack of education, makes it difficult for many families to adopt ecologically sound techniques. Also, the proliferation of private entrepreneurs seeking quick profits by any methods is now an increasing threat to the environment.

There has been progressive depletion of natural forest, with remaining areas owing much to their relative inaccessibility. Deforestation causes local degradation and exaggerates the effects of both drought and floods. China has a number of major projects designed to increase tree cover. For example, large-scale planting has been helping to protect the loess lands and establish a 'Great Wall' of trees across northern China, with considerable success on the northern plains. There are also plans to establish a coastal forest, and tree-belt along the middle and lower Chang jiang. However, all these projects are aimed primarily at

protecting cultivated areas and providing large shelter belts, rather than establishing forest reserves. In the cities a long standing 'citizen tree-planting programme' has helped to green many urban areas, despite the increasing spread of concrete buildings.

China has many hundreds of protected vertebrate and plant species, and receives international co-operation in this through UNESCO's Biosphere and World Heritage programmes. There are numerous nature reserves, varying in size and efficiency: the Wolong Reserve in Sichuan is the largest of those protecting the giant panda and has its own district government, though even there illicit logging is a problem. To help fund such reserves visits by tourists are being encouraged, though it is recognised that tourism is not always environmentally friendly.

Water shortage and water pollution are now major problems. With increasing demands, many lakes and reservoirs have been shrinking. There is also inefficient use of water in agriculture and lack of recycling in most manufacturing industries. With a growing population and more homes with modern plumbing, demands for water are

Figure 6.23 Millions of young trees now protect soils in the loess lands. In summer these will help to conserve moisture supplied by irrigation from the pump-house on the right

Figure 6.22 *(far left)* Many of the hills in eastern Yunnan are being stripped bare of forest. Only the most careful contouring can prevent erosion on the scale of that seen in Figure 6.24

Figure 6.24 *(right)* Badland erosion in denuded hillsides adjacent to those seen in Figure 6.22 – a warning to those planning to increase settlement in the south west (page 65)

likely to go on rising. In densely populated areas groundwater levels are falling, particularly rapidly in Shanghai and in Tianjin, as well as in other large regional cities such as Nanning and Kunming.

The water quality of rivers has also deteriorated through additions of industrial wastes, untreated sewage, and runoff from farmland receiving large amounts of fertilisers. Also many estuaries and bays now receive high quantities of organic wastes from sewage and heavy metals from factories, including the Bohai Gulf, the Pearl River estuary and Hangzhou Bay. Shanghai, aided by the World Bank, now has a system to discharge sewage into the East China Sea; though unfortunately this provides nutrients for organisms and creates 'tides' of red plankton which are harmful to other marine life.

As water shortage is particularly severe in and about the northern cities, there are long term plans for inter-basin transfers, such as extending the use of the Grand Canal as a conduit and pumping water northwards from the Chang jiang. Eventually water from the Three Gorges Reservoir may supply the north via stores in Henan.

Though not suffering the severe water shortages of the north, the south is experiencing a loss of soil fertility through an increase in triple-cropping especially with rice

monoculture. The use of so much water encourages **gleying**, since a lack of oxygen reduces bacterial action and leaves ferrous iron compounds in a blue-grey clayey layer in the soil. Elsewhere inexpert farmers, who now seek to maximise output, are affecting soil fertility through over-application of organic and chemical fertilisers. Thus the ability of the nation to feed itself is threatened both by increasing population and soil losses through various forms of degradation.

Coal, the main source of energy for factories, and used in inefficient domestic furnaces, often has a high sulphur content. The increasing acidity of the summer rainfall is particularly likely to affect soils in the south east, most of which are naturally acidic. Efforts are being made with varying success to reduce air pollution in urban areas throughout the country and to provide suitable fuels and chemical filters.

The Government has found that the management of manufacturing enterprises has often been lax in the use of pollution control equipment; and that wasteful uses of water, coal and timber have been partly due to under-pricing. Priorities to combat environmental deterioration therefore include population control, environmental education, price regulation, funding improvements in marginal areas and obtaining foreign support for large-scale projects.

Figure 6.25 Sulphurous emissions pour over inner Beijing, with particles adding to the fine dust carried from the west during winter. The campaign for cleaner air and urban 'greening' is having an effect, but many northern cities suffer serious air pollution.

In Focus ....

● Why is rapid economic development generally accompanied by environmental deterioration?

● In China which types of chemical pollution may result from: the opportunity for 'get-rich-quick' farming; the release with no treatment of 80 per cent of the water used; and the disposal of local industrial wastes. Suggest why, as yet, so many fail to appreciate this, or are unable to deal with it.

Facing the future

Figure 6.27 A machine-tool factory in Kunming – the participation of women in manufacturing has increased with the economic transformation of the rural economy, family planning policies, and opportunities in non-state enterprises

Population increase

The size and growth rate of the population in China are issues which will affect progress in many ways. There will be 1300 million people by the year 2000, with signs of relaxing fertility control and a tendency towards earlier marriage. This alone will make it difficult to maintain food grain production per capita at the present level and, in addition, agricultural land is being lost to commercial development. Also consumption is rising with better living standards and improving diets, and so either yields will have to increase or China will become increasingly dependent on imported grain. Even with greater investment in agriculture, possible improvements in seed varieties and further land reclamation it seems likely that China's future demands on world markets will be considerable.

With growing population and increasing urbanisation, there are already problems in providing employment, even though new enterprises are being created. Foreign firms are likely to continue their interest in a huge market which is raising its living standards, but despite foreign investment the state still has to finance new projects to provide employment. At the same time they must either provide huge amounts for welfare benefits or continue to maintain inefficient state units which themselves provide welfare amenities.

Channelling foreign inputs

Political stability is needed to ensure that foreign capital will continue to be available. There will be no lack of interest by companies across the globe, for though relatively few Chinese are becoming 'wealthy' the potential market is enormous, and there are now frequent official trade missions from European countries, including the UK.

Continuing the economic surge of the coastal zones is still a priority, but it is also essential to channel investment towards the interior to redress the growing imbalance. Highly attractive tax incentives are already helping to establish large enterprises inland, and the effects on cities like Urumqi have been noted in Part 5, although the bulk of investment continues to pour into the coastal regions.

Provincial disparities

Regional coastal development aimed at opening doors to western Pacific neighbours and overseas investors has produced economically strong zones – the Bohai rim, the central corridor-delta 'T', and the South East. Within these zones certain provinces have become powerful enough to take actions which tend to undermine those of the central Government. There has been manipulation of central tax collection, a proportion of which goes to central Government (which subsidises minority regions and poorer

Figure 6.26 Business activities in central Shenzhen with its banks, offices and super-stores

Figure 6.28 Night-time taxis streaming past illuminated hotels and stores in central Shanghai

Figure 6.29 Eighty per cent of China's population is rural. Their responses to the seasons, the daily routines of village life and journeys to the local market are far removed from the China of high-rise flats and the increasing sophistication of life in the big cities

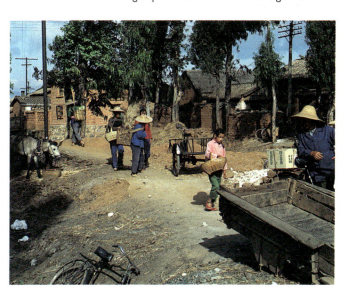

provinces). Provinces can also impose provincial taxes, designed to meet their own needs. Thus strong provinces, like Guangdong, have begun to establish projects and finance construction which may, or may not, be considered a national priority.

The difficulty is that putting a brake on financial independence of a go-ahead province may suppress the economic development of which it is capable and which China needs. Moves to regional independence of the kind that occurred in the former USSR are unlikely, but the extent of decision making at provincial level is a political issue.

Central control or liberalisation

With the open market system and very rapid economic growth have come social problems. Responses to high inflation and unfamiliar rises in the cost of living led to protests which were partly responsible for creating the 1989 disturbances and the ensuing drastic state intervention. Also, increasing freedoms and individual enrichment have brought a degree of corruption which could not have existed under the previous rigid central control. This in itself makes it difficult for more liberal policies to be maintained free from repressions.

In weighing up and comparing economic problems under the Commune system and the consequences of present liberalisation with strong central controls, it is easy to ignore the benefits which both systems have brought to millions of families over the years, albeit with periods of disruption. For the population as a whole, life expectancy has doubled, and far exceeds that of most developing countries. There have recently been remarkable increases in income and ownership of consumer durables. Treasured possessions

have moved from thermos flask, cycle, wristwatch and sewing machine to television, washing machine and refrigerator. Regional disparities remain, of course as do the remarkable contrasts in lifestyle and daily activities within China's population.

With its natural resources and population, China has the potential to become one of the strong industrialising countries of Eastern Asia, and a government with authoritative central control has certainly helped in the case of other Newly Industrialising Countries (NICs) such as Taiwan, Singapore and South Korea. Within the next few decades, with Hong Kong absorbed, stability at home, and with the co-operation of powerful neighbours, China could become an economic giant.

In Focus ....

- It has been stressed that China's future progress depends on internal stability. Consider in more detail how each of the following might act to threaten stability over the new few decades: ethnic differences; the ageing population; personal mobility; physical and economic imbalance between regions; opportunities for illicit activities; and Government efforts to curb the latter.

Appendix

Glossary

bureaucracy a hierarchical system of government by officials responsible to the official above

cadre a person in a position of official authority

co-operative a group working together to better achieve economic advantage

ethnic concerning a particular racial group with its own culture and customs

fertility rate the number of births per fertile woman (in China in 1963 averaging 7.5, falling to 2.4 by 1985, with only slight fluctuations to 1995)

geothermal energy derived from the internal heat of the earth

gleying waterlogging leading to soil oxygen deficiency, reducing the red-brown ferric iron content to blue-grey ferrous iron, with a clayey texture.

hi-tech industry one employing highly skilled workers on technical processes (often involving micro-electronics)

intermediate technology using improved equipment, affordable, and appropriate to the skills of a developing society, preferably available from local sources

karez irrigation using water brought from water-bearing strata through sub-surface tunnels and raised to the surface where needed

karst an area of cavernous limestone reduced mainly by solution, with underlying drainage and remnant blocks, peaks, and pinnacles

open policy a strategy to encourage participation in the world market, with technology transfers and foreign direct investment

polje a closed solution hollow in a karst region, long and flat-bottomed

push/pull influence (on migration) 'push' impelling people to leave an unsatisfactory environment: 'pull' the attractions of economic opportunities and social conditions (real or imagined) which a new location offers

primary industry obtaining raw materials (agriculture, forestry, fishing, mining)

secondary industry concerned with the processing and manufacturing of raw materials

tertiary industry concerned with providing a service

township enterprise a business not directly agricultural run at a township; most now operate according to market forces

urbanisation whereby an increasing proportion of the population in an area becomes concentrated in towns and cities, also an increase in the number and size of towns

yurt a tent of skins on a portable framework

Place names

Most place names are descriptive of locations, whether physical feature (Changsha – long sandbank); climate (Yunnan – south of the clouds); mood (Yanan – peaceful River Yan); or notability (Longmen – dragon gate). The following translations give meaning to many place names referred to in the text. There can be misinterpretation, which is why Xian city is often written Xi'an, to indicate 'western peace' rather than county status. However, in general, translation can turn the unfamiliar into the helpful, and Qinhuangdao changes from an awkward name for a major port to an historical location – 'the island of the first Qin emperor'.

Natural features

water	shui
river	he, jiang, pu, shui
ocean, sea	hai
gulf, bay	wan
creek	hezi
harbour, port	gang
lake	chi, hu, nur, po
island	dao
canal	yunhe
channel	zhen
sandbank	sha
stone	shi
mountain	shan
range	ling
peak	feng
valley	gu
pass	guan
basin	pendi
desert	shamo
forest	lin
cassia tree	gui
cloud(s)	yu, yun

Colour

black	hei
white	bai
blue	lan
green	lu, qing
red	hong
yellow	huang

Direction

north	bei
south	nan
east	dong
west	xi
back	hou
front	qian
deep	shen
high	tai
right	you
left	zuo
central	zhong
inner	nei
outer	wai

Association/Location

peace	an
great	da, tai
little	xiao
broad (extensive)	guang
long	chang
dragon	long
Buddha	Fo
place, region	zhou
city	shi
county	xian
province	sheng
town, village	cunzhen
town (admin.)	xiaug, zhen

Index